A Jill Norman Book

Published in Great Britain in 1986 by
Dorling Kindersley Publishers Limited,
9 Henrietta Street, London WC2E 8PS

British Library Cataloguing in Publication Data
Olney, Richard
   Yquem.
   1. Sauternes – History 2. Wine and wine making
   – France – Château d'Yquem Lur Saluces
   – History
   I. Title
   641.2'222'094471 TP553
   ISBN 0-86318-180-5

Printed in Switzerland
by Imprimeries Réunies de Lausanne

RICHARD OLNEY

PREFACE BY
MICHAEL BROADBENT

Y Q U E M

PHOTOGRAPHS
MICHEL GUILLARD

DESIGNER
MARC WALTER

DORLING KINDERSLEY

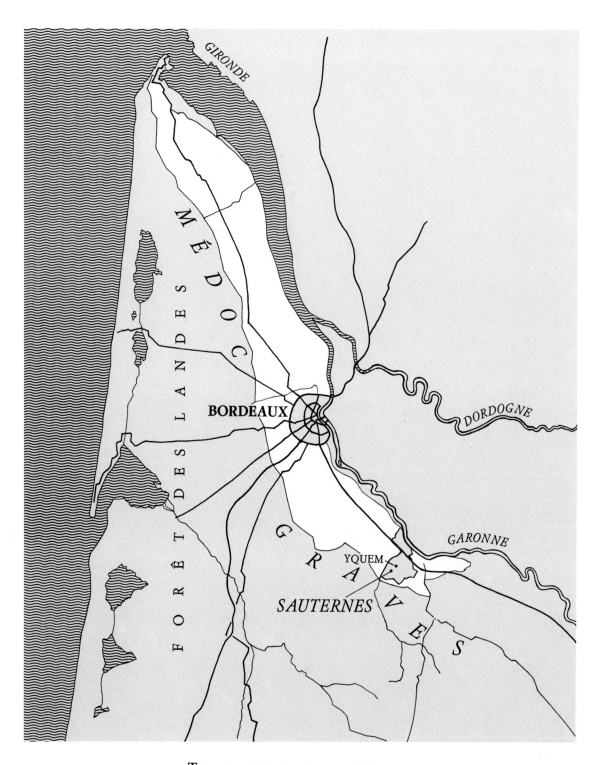

The region of Médoc, Graves and Sauternes.

The château in the autumnal morning mist, atmospheric condition vital to Yquem's perfection (preceding pages).

C O N T E N T S

Preface by Michael Broadbent	9
Foreword	11
Four Centuries of History	15
Château d'Yquem Today	27
Noble Rot	39
The Genius of the Soil	51
Yquem and the Great Vineyard Crises	61
Works and Days	73
Vintage and Vinification	89
Yquem and the Table	125
Collectors, Tastings and Vintages	147
The Most Expensive Wine in the World Is Not Expensive	159
Notes	161
Bibliography	164
Acknowledgements	165

To the comte and the comtesse
de Lur Saluces

THE TASTE
OF PURE GOLD

Living as we do in an age of rushing to cut corners, of insidious commercial pressures and of the marketing man's goal, tastelessness, we should pause and give thanks to a product which blithely carries on as if the latter part of the twentieth century did not exist.

Yquem can justifiably claim to be the greatest white wine in the world. Its fame was fully established by the middle of the eighteenth century. It was a favourite at the Courts of the tsars and of America's first connoisseur, Thomas Jefferson, who put it at the top of his list of great white wines, seeking out the renowned 1784 and subsequent vintages.

Continuity of ownership has something to do with it. Coincidentally those two great German wine " châteaux ", Schloss Johannisberg and Schloss Vollrads have also prospered under the benevolent continuity of aristocratic proprietors, and each makes a glorious golden-sweet wine from over-ripe grapes affected with noble rot. The German proprietors however, have an advantage : their grapes are harvested in stages to make several styles and qualities of wine. They can afford the risk – and the luxury – of leaving a few bunches of grapes on the vines if there is a chance that the climatic conditions towards the end of the vintage are likely to be conducive to the development of noble rot.

At Yquem, as at all the châteaux in the Sauternes district, it is all or nothing. If the mid-autumn weather changes for the worse, the entire crop can be ruined. They have no early-picked grapes to provide bread-and-butter wines. But these risks are more fully explained by Richard Olney. All I might emphasize in my preface is that the vineyards have to be tended, throughout the year, no matter what the weather and no matter what the outcome. Quality and quantity are in the lap of the gods, and somehow the cost must be spread over a longer period than just one vintage. Painstaking work, a meticulous eye for detail with no expense spared, the constant hovering year-in-year-out risk of disaster, must inevitably result in an expensive bottle of wine. But what glorious stuff it is!

Over the past thirty-odd years I have been privileged to taste – in fact to drink – even I do not spit out nectar – no fewer than sixty vintages of Yquem, the oldest being the fabled 1784 tasted in the company of Alexandre de Lur Saluces at one of Hardy Rodenstock's remarkable fine and rare wine " happenings ". This was in the autumn of 1985. The wine had never been recorked. It had none of the faults of old age, being neither oxidised nor pricked with acidity; it was just perfect. But this is one of the extraordinary qualities of Yquem: its uncanny ability to remain sound and drinkable no matter what its age and, sometimes, no matter what its appearance. Rodenstock's previous tasting, in 1984, also featured a group of vintages of Yquem, the most memorable of which was also the most unlikely. Coincidentally, just a century younger than the " Jefferson " vintage just referred to, this 1884 Yquem was extraordinary. I clearly recall its glorious mid-gold/amber colour with a hint of rust; above all its extraordinary orange-blossom-and-honey bouquet which assailed the nostrils and held, without fading, in the glass for twelve hours; still sweet, soft, creamy and with perfect acidity. You see, it was not even of a notably great year, yet, tasted exactly one hundred years to the month after the vintage in which it was made, it was still full of character and pure delight.

There are some who say that such-and-such a château produces comparable wine; that in certain vintages Yquem can be matched or even topped, the implication being that Yquem is perhaps overrated and over-priced. All I can say is that this sort of talk is specious, often mischievous and, in my experience, not borne out by tasting. Somehow, even though another first growth Sauternes might have, in a given vintage, all the component parts to make a great wine, Yquem when tasted alongside always presents an extra dimension: greater intensity, perfume, length, aftertaste.

I salute Yquem. I admire the qualities of the family which, at considerable sacrifice of time, effort and money, strives only for the best. My old friend Richard Olney and his publishers have produced a fitting tribute to both the family and the wine.

Michael Broadbent
Christie's, London 1986

FOREWORD

On the sixth day of June 1785, at Château d'Yquem, Louis-Amédée de Lur Saluces, godson of Louis XV and a colonel in the Penthièvre-dragons regiment, and Françoise-Joséphine de Sauvage, " dame d'Yquem, de Podensac, de Saint-Criq, etc. ", whose family had been at Yquem since the sixteenth century, were united in marriage. Thus four centuries of history are united in the spare legend, " Château d'Yquem Lur-Saluces ", which accompanied by a vintage date, comprises the most discreet of all wine labels [1] – a label that carries but one association the world over, that of a luminous amber essence, so rich that it pours more slowly and more silently than other wines ...

Yquem is an enchanted realm, somewhere outside of time, in which the comte and the comtesse de Lur Saluces receive professors and princes, artists, doctors, collectors, ambassadors of nations and of wine, all impassioned Yquem fanciers, in an atmosphere whose only bias is that of viticulture and vinification. The conversation turns upon the art of making the vine suffer to give its best, and the mysterious powers of the mould called noble rot, upon the *éclat* of Yquem's sparkling golden robe and upon the nuances of its bouquet.

The tsars of Russia were loyal clients and, more recently, Joseph Stalin's admiration for Yquem was such that he begged the marquis Bertrand de Lur Saluces to send him cuttings of the vines, so that he might extract this miraculous nectar from Russian terrain ! On Yquem's office walls faded photographs crowd in upon one another, memories

The comte and the comtesse Alexandre de Lur Saluces.

of visits by personalities as diverse as Josephine Baker and the Lord Mayor of London and, in its visitors books, the signatures of Alfonso XIII, King of Spain, and his suite vie with those of members of the Russian Imperial Guard and of celebrities from the worlds of the arts and the sciences.

In homage to a great wine and to the Lur Saluces family, in celebration of its bicentenary presence at Château d'Yquem, I have tried to bring into focus the miracle of Yquem and to illuminate the uncommon circumstances that have rendered it a symbol of perfection. It is born of the genius of the soil, it is the microclimate that permits the proliferation of noble rot, conferring upon the wine its distinctive taste, but it is the rigid respect for the traditions and the ethics of vinification and the fastidious care with which the wine is raised that ensure its uniqueness and long life. Yquem's exalted reputation and its place at the world's most celebrated tables, past and present, are the mundane facets of its being, without which all of the other factors would be helpless to work their magic.

Talleyrand's observation to Louis XVIII, that he had a greater need for saucepans than for written instructions, could as well have been said of the wine cellar. For two centuries Yquem's liquorous and seductive talents have served the ends of diplomacy at royal, presidential and ambassadorial tables, most often hand-in-hand with the princely turbot. George Washington stocked the first presidential cellar of the United States with Yquem of the 1787 vintage on the advice of his ambassador to France, Thomas Jefferson, who had earlier been swayed by the beauty of the 1784 ; Yquem's cellar books record consignments, mostly of the 1802 vintage, to " S.M. L'empereur " during the years of Napoleon's glory ; it is a recurrent presence on menus from all the courts of Europe and on those of the Elysée Palace when receiving crowned heads ; Prince Charles drank Yquem at his marriage and Ronald Reagan served Yquem to François Mitterrand …

The renown of Bordeaux's great growths and their classification within a hierarchical structure of different levels of *noblesse* was firmly, if unofficially, established by the end of the eighteenth century. What had been accepted tradition became official dogma in 1855 when, at the request of the Bordeaux Chamber of Commerce, the Bordeaux winebrokers' syndicate prepared separate classifications of the red and white wines of the Gironde for the presentation of Bordeaux's wines at the Paris world fair of that year. The red wines were divided into first, second, third, fourth and fifth *crus* or growths, of which four properties were distinguished as *premiers crus*. The white wines, all from the Sauternes region and encompassing the communities of Sauternes, Fargues, Preignac, Bommes and Barsac, were divided into first and second growths, with the exception of Yquem whose supremacy was consecrated with the unique and unchallenged classification of *premier cru supérieur*.

Even before tasting Yquem, this dazzling liquid which seems to radiate its own light from within inspires wonder. And, having tasted it, the troubling sense of the wine's embodying something very ancient – a mystery that one can divine but cannot express – plagues one's rational being for want of lucid description. Exclamations like " A ray of sunshine in a glass ! " or " The extravagance of perfection ! " do not bring us much closer to understanding the wine.

The problem is that we have no criterion for comparison; Yquem, the yardstick by which other Sauternes are measured, is its own frame of reference. Its qualities of sweetness, of bitterness and of fruit are not the sweetness, the bitterness and the fruits that we know. If it is often helplessly likened to honey, almonds and peaches, that is only because the sweetness and the fruits that we find there we have never tasted elsewhere.

On the palate, it has a voluptuous texture and, at the same time, a sort of crystalline vibrance that strikes memories of the clear notes of certain musical instruments; its structure, to be sure, is that of architecture – more precise analogies would be dangerous.

It is long-lived – twenty, fifty, a hundred years and more. And its colour shifts in time, as from dawn to dusk, from glistening straw to burnished gold, amber, caramel hues and transluscent mahogany.

Yquem is a wine for celebration, a wine for anniversaries and fêtes; it is a wine for ritual occasions and for those – best of all – on which friends, bound by a common passion, simply gather together at table. Jean-Pierre Haeberlin (l'Auberge de l'Ill, Illhaeusern) shared a magnum of 1937 with friends to celebrate his fiftieth birthday and Alain Chapel (Mionnay) drank the same vintage at his fortieth; Georges Blanc (La Mère Blanc, Vonnas) cherishes the memory of a 1921 shared with clients and Pierre Wynants (Comme Chez Soi, Brussels) uncorks a bottle of Yquem for each of his family's anniversaries. To celebrate the near-completion of the *Yquem* manuscript, Ghislaine Bavoillot, the French publisher's food and wine editor, a few friends and I crowned a sublime luncheon at Hiély, in Avignon, with a 1904 Yquem ...

Louis Outhier (L'Oasis, La Napoule) recounts a childhood memory that exquisitely defines the awe and respect which Yquem commands in a traditional French family of comfortable but not extraordinary means.

"My memory of Yquem is a childhood memory. In a corner of my parent's cellar, an ancient metal wine rack, the only one with a door. It creaked but once a year, on Christmas Eve, to release a single bottle. It was a bottle of Yquem that would accompany the foie gras, prepared by my mother for the occasion. A ritual ceremony by candlelight was enacted to remove the bottle, with infinite care, from its niche in the rack. The caress of an old shaving brush swept the thick layer of dust from its blazon, reinstating its identity before the bottle reappeared in the light of the dining room, charged with festive fragrances. The vintage I know not, but the memory of its golden amber colour and the fact that this door opened but once a year makes me think that it must have been a rarity. Tasting, exaltation, comments and dithyrambic epithets always finishing with my father's exclamation 'It is Yquem that should bear the name of Lacryma Christi!'."

> ... there was not one amongst them who would not have thought it a breach
> of respect to the duc and the duchesse
> were a ball to be given without my name figuring on the list,
> and at the same time, while drinking one of the Yquems
> concealed in the Guermantes cellars, I savoured ortolans ...
> (Marcel Proust),
> *A la Recherche du Temps Perdu*

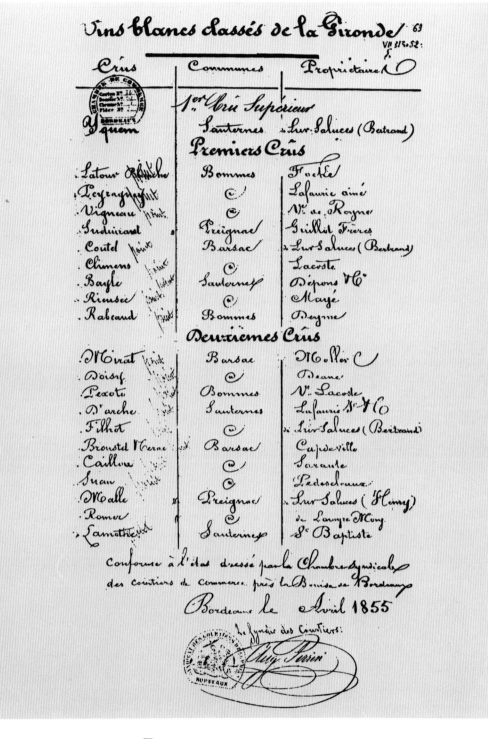

The 1855 official classification of the white wines of the Gironde.

FOUR CENTURIES OF HISTORY

The property of Yquem, part of the Royal Provostship of Barsac, belonged to the kings of England, dukes of Aquitaine, from the time of Eleanor d'Aquitaine's marriage to Henry Plantagenet in 1152, until it passed into the hands of the kings of France in 1453, during Charles VII's reign, nearly a century and a half before the Sauvage family's tenure.

How the property came to be named " Yquem " or " Iquem " is unknown. Etymologists trace the origins of the word to the Germanic *aig-helm* (*aigan :* to have ; *helm :* helmet or casque). From these same origins sprang *Aichelmus, Akelmus, Ayquelmus* and *Ayquem,* all common first names in Guienne from the tenth century onwards. Today, *Eyquem,* a spelling dating from the sixteenth century, is a common Bordeaux family name, derived from these archaic Christian names.

The origin of the Montaigne Myth lies in the mere similarity of these names and that of Yquem. The reiterated claim that Yquem is in some way – never clearly defined – allied to the family of the celebrated sixteenth-century essayist, Michel Eyquem de Montaigne, is absolutely unfounded.

To confuse the issue and to reinforce the claim to a Montaigne connection, several authors have also insisted that the Lur Saluces are directly descended from Montaigne. This would seem to be a deliberate misreading of the family's genealogy. In 1600, Honoré de Lur Saluces, aged 6, was married to Françoise de la Tour d'Eviez, aged 9, daughter of Elénonore de Montaigne, Michel de Montaigne's daughter. Their only son died in battle leaving no descendants. It was from Honoré de Lur Saluces's second marriage that Claude-Honoré de Lur Saluces was born to continue the line. In short, Montaigne was neither allied in any way to Yquem in the past, nor does his blood flow in the Lur Saluces's veins at present.

The Sauvage d'Yquem family name disappeared with Laurent de Sauvage d'Yquem, " colonel d'infanterie, chevalier de l'ordre royal et militaire de Saint-Louis ", whose only child, Françoise-Joséphine, by her marriage to comte Louis-Amédée de Lur Saluces, transferred the Yquem inheritance to the Lur Saluces patrimony. Traces of the family in Bordeaux reach back to the mid-fourteenth century when Aquitaine was under English rule. At the time of King Edward III's reign, Roger Sauvage was mayor of Bordeaux. During the last quarter of the fourteenth century, Arnaut Sauvage was governor of Gascony and, in the 1380s, Pierre Sauvage and Jean Sauvage both appear as provosts of Barsac. Members of the family are repeatedly mentioned in the " Rôles Gascons "[2] between the years 1352 and 1440.

A marble plaque at the Château d'Armajan-des-Ormes in Preignac, dated 1566, commemorates Pierre de Sauvage's ennoblement, following a visit by the young King Charles IX, the queen mother Catherine de Medici and their court in 1565.

By a deed dated 8 December 1593, Pierre's nephew, Jacques de Sauvage, " conseiller du roi et son trésorier général en la généralité establye en Guienne ", acquired tenant's rights to the royal property holdings of Yquem[3].

A certain confusion surrounds Jacques's activities. J. Barennes, archivist and paleographer, refers to him as Jacques de Sauvage, seigneur d'Armajan (having just quoted a legal document dated 1585 which defines Pierre's son, Jean, as " seigneur of the noble houses of Armajan and of Lamothe, in Preignac, only son of the late seigneur de Sauvage and of demoiselle Jeanne de Los ") and cites Jacques's will, 1609, in which his three children by his deceased wife, Marie de la Roche – François, Ramond and Marie – are disinherited, his properties being bestowed upon his nephews, while his second wife is named usufructuary at Yquem.

The reasons for the disinheritance of these " children by flesh and procreation but not by obedience " were as follows : François, the eldest son, refused to marry the girl of his father's choice having contracted another marriage against his father's wishes ; Marie, a widow, had allowed herself to be abducted by a young man ; finally, Ramond was disinherited for having approved and aided his sister and her abductor. The loyal brother and disobedient youngest son must have been received back into the family by his stepmother, for it was he who was to continue holding the feudal tenancy at Yquem.

According to L'Armorial du Bordelais (1906), the (de) Sauvage family received its letters of nobility in the seventeenth century ; no distinction is made between Pierre de Sauvage and the Sauvage d'Yquem line descended from Pierre's brother Bernard – they are listed not only as " seigneurs d'Yquem, Podensac, Saint-Cricq, etc ", but also of " Armajan " and " La Mothe ". These papers have disappeared from the Yquem archives, presumably in the public conflagrations of the Revolution, but François de Sauvage, Ramond's son, is known to have been actively royalist at the time of " La Fronde " and " l'Ormée "[4], when the Bordelais generally supported the opposition, and to have been recompensed by Louis XIV for his loyalty. If it was at this time that the Sauvage d'Yquem family was ennobled, it can probably be dated around 1654, the year of François's marriage.

François's children are depicted in a naïve mural painting, dated 1664, above the mantelpiece of a fireplace at Yquem. Beneath each child is printed an age : 7 ans (girl) ;

*Fresco above a fireplace
in the château representing
François de Sauvage's children.*

Eutrope-Alexandre de Lur Saluces.

*Laurent de Sauvage,
Françoise-Joséphine's father.*

2 *ans* (boy) ; 5 *ans* (girl) ; 8 *ans* (boy). The 8-year-old boy with the greyhound is Léon de Sauvage, Françoise-Joséphine's great grandfather.

The Sauvage family remained tenants until 1711 when Yquem became their fiefdom. This transaction is illuminated by a note delivered to the comtesse Françoise-Joséphine by the local authorities in the years following the Revolution : " Memorandum for Mme de Lur Saluces concerning the domain of Yquem situated in the communities of Sauternes, Bommes and Preignac. Rental rights of common origin – The noble property rights purchased by M. Léon d'Yquem according to the Council's decision of 18 September 1708 and of the Treasury of France, 31 August 1711 ".

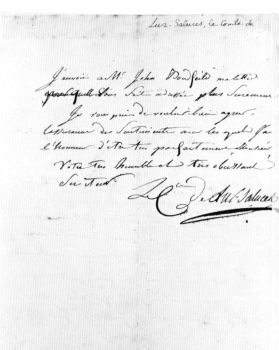

On 16 July 1711, Léon de Sauvage purchased the " enfranchisement of the king's rents ", " in consideration of which the administrators declared that, in the future, he would hold and possess his property nobly ... ". He registered the bill of sale with the office of the " Trésoriers de France " on 31 August.

The history of the Lur Saluces family consists of an unending succession of noble warriors, many of whose lives were cut short in battle while serving the kings of France. Letters from Charles IX, Henri III and the Bourbon kings all attest to their valour and their loyalty to the royal cause.

Originally Franconian, the Lur family was established in the Limousin by the tenth century. In 1472, Pierre de Lur, baron de Malengin, married Izabelle de Montferrand, " vicomtesse d'Uza, dame de Fargues, Belin, Aureilhan, etc. ". Uza, a vast forest domain

*Letter dated 7 January 1788 from
comte Louis-Amédée de Lur Saluces to Thomas Jefferson.*

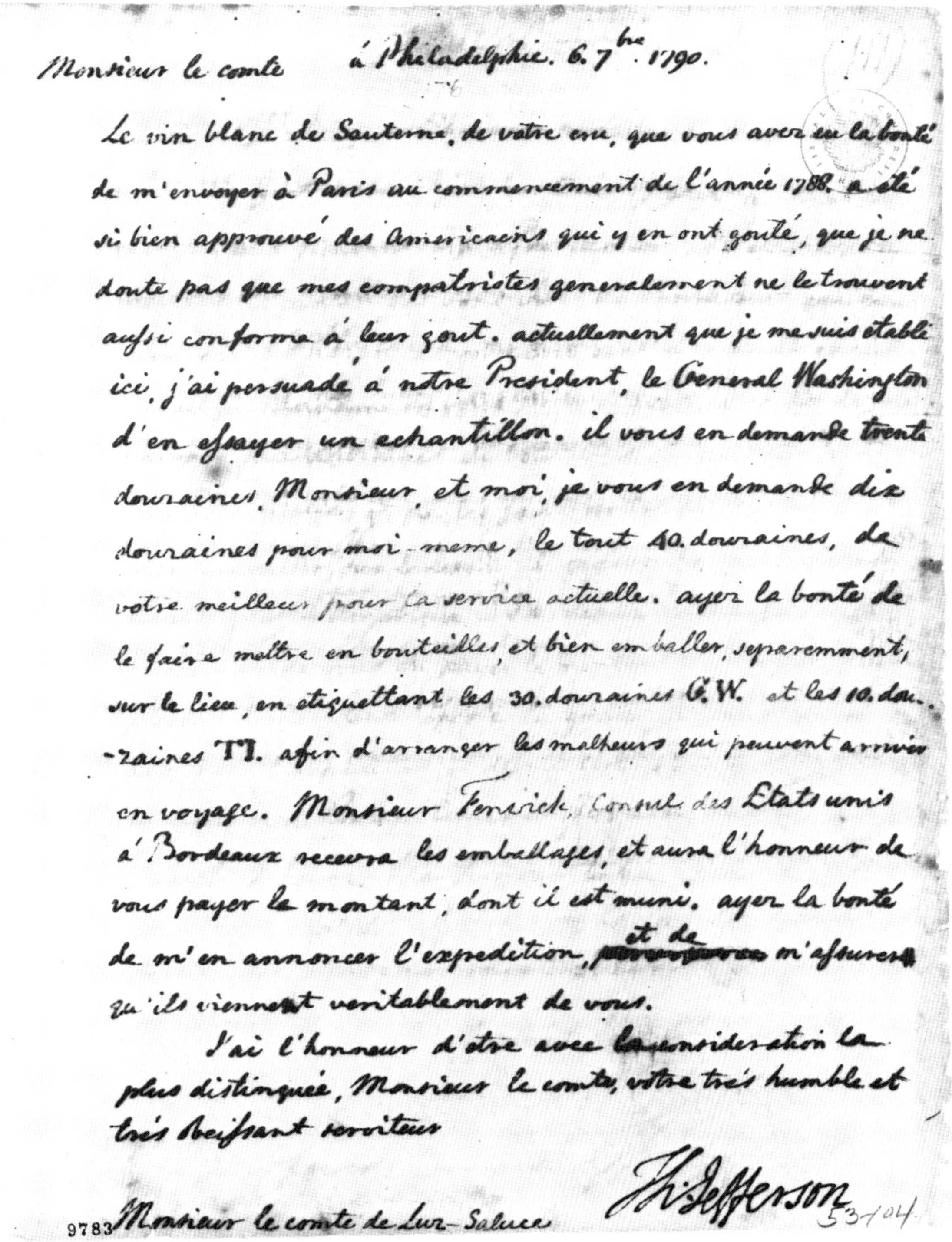

Monsieur le comte   à Philadelphie. 6. 7bre. 1790.

Le vin blanc de Sauterne, de vôtre cru, que vous avez eu la bonté
de m'envoyer à Paris au commencement de l'année 1788. a été
si bien approuvé des Americains qui y en ont gouté, que je ne
doute pas que mes compatriotes generalement ne le trouvent
aussi conforme à leur gout. actuellement que je me suis etabli
ici, j'ai persuadé à nôtre President, le General Washington
d'en essayer un echantillon. il vous en demande trente
douzaines, Monsieur, et moi, je vous en demande dix
douzaines pour moi-meme, le tout 40. douzaines, de
vôtre meilleur pour le service actuelle. ayez la bonté de
le faire mettre en bouteilles, et bien emballer, separemment,
sur le lieu, en etiquettant les 30. douzaines G. W. et les 10. dou-
-zaines TJ. afin d'arranger les malheurs qui peuvent arriver
en voyage. Monsieur Fenwick, Consul des Etats unis
à Bordeaux recevra les emballages, et aura l'honneur de
vous payer le montant, dont il est muni. ayez la bonté
de m'en annoncer l'expedition, et de m'assurer
qu'ils viennent veritablement de vous.

        J'ai l'honneur d'etre avec la consideration la
plus distinguée, Monsieur le comte, vôtre tres humble et
tres obeissant serviteur

                                        Th: Jefferson

Monsieur le comte de Luz-Saluces

Letter dated 6 September 1790 from Thomas Jefferson,
then United States ambassador to the court of Versailles.

19

in the Landes, and the domain of Fargues, a stone's throw from Yquem, are still in the Lur Saluces family; they and the Sauvages were neighbours for a least two centuries before the marriage of comte Louis-Amédée and Françoise-Joséphine de Sauvage.

The Lurs were joined to the Saluces in 1586 by the marriage of Jean, great-grandson of Pierre, to Charlotte-Catherine de Saluces, only child of Auguste, marquis de Saluces and last of his line, whose father, Jean-Louis, had been the last sovereign marquis of Saluces and of Montferrat.

In his daughter's marriage contract, Auguste de Saluces inserted a clause stipulating that her second child should "bear the name and the arms of Saluces". The first Lur Saluces was Honoré, the child bridegroom of Françoise de la Tour d'Eviez.

The Château de Fargues was built in 1306 (by Cardinal Raymond de Fargues, a nephew of Pope Clément V, whose name is still borne by the vineyard in Graves); in it six generations of Lurs and Lur Saluces were born before it burnt down in 1687. Today it is a spectacular and melancholy ruin of ragged walls devoured by ivy, still climbable remnants of circular staircases, missing floors and upper-storey fireplaces hung eerily in silent space beneath the open sky.

In 1702, the marriage of Eutrope-Alexandre, second son of the last generation to be born at Fargues, brought Château de Malle (Preignac) into the family, where it remained until 1937, passing by inheritance through comte Louis-Amédée's two younger brothers, united in a single branch during the nineteenth century by a marriage of cousins.

On 29 October 1788, on the eve of the Revolution and only three years after his marriage, comte Louis-Amédée de Lur Saluces died at the parish of Saint-Jacques-du-Haut-Pas in Paris, where he had been transported after being thrown from a horse at the military camp of Saint-Omer[5], leaving a 2-year-old son, Antoine-Marie (the only Lur Saluces to be born at Yquem). Louis-Amédée's father, the marquis Claude-Henry de Lur Saluces, Field Marshal in the king's armies, was condemned to death for royalist sympathies by the revolutionary tribunal of Bordeaux on 14 December 1793. One brother had emigrated to Spain (on his father's advice "because Spain was the power in whose service he would be the least likely to have to take up arms against his own country", and the other one

*Françoise-Joséphine de Sauvage, dame d'Yquem,
comtesse de Lur Saluces.*

was briefly imprisoned in Bordeaux. The following document, dated 11 December, three days before the marquis Claude-Henry's trial, speaks for itself : " Authority given to citizen Jean Garros by Mᵉ Françoise Josephine d'Iquem to visit the papers that are in the house of Iquem, and this in the presence of the Sauternes municipality, if it should see fit, in order, after having sorted out the feudal papers, to hand them over to the clerk's office of the said community ". A paper dated the following day, " à Sauternes le 23 frimaire de l'an 2 ", certifies that all " titles, feudal or seigneurial papers " have been delivered to the municipality of Sauternes and that they have, " in accordance with the law, been burned publicly in the square of the said community ".

On 26 December, two weeks later, an inventory – the first step in the confiscation of a property – signed by the mayors of Preignac and Sauternes, was taken of " effects belonging to Lur Saluces to be found on the premises of Yquem ". Finally, a petition dated 9 March 1794, addressed by Madame de Lur Saluces to " the citizen representative for the people, in session at Bordeaux ", requests that the sale of her possessions be adjourned ...

The stages of the rough road that the young comtesse travelled during these years are thrown into uncertain focus by a paucity of documents. That repeated attempts were made to wrest the property from her seems certain ; she was imprisoned for a time but precisely when, or for how long, is unclear. The fact that at the beginning of the nineteenth century she was addressing herself to the local authorities in search of the origins of her proprietorship, strongly suggests that usurping aspirants, convinced that her rights were of a feudal nature, revoked by the Revolution, were still on the scene. The proof of her great-grandfather's purchase of the property undoubtedly rescued Yquem, to which she was fiercely attached and where she remained until her death in 1851 at the age of 83.

The marriage of her son, marquis Antoine-Marie, in 1807 brought Château Coutet (Barsac) and Château Filhot (Sauternes) into the family patrimony (Coutet was sold in

Marquis Romain-Bertrand de Lur Saluces,
his son, Eugène, and his grandsons,
Bertrand and Amédée, comte Alexandre's father (left to right).

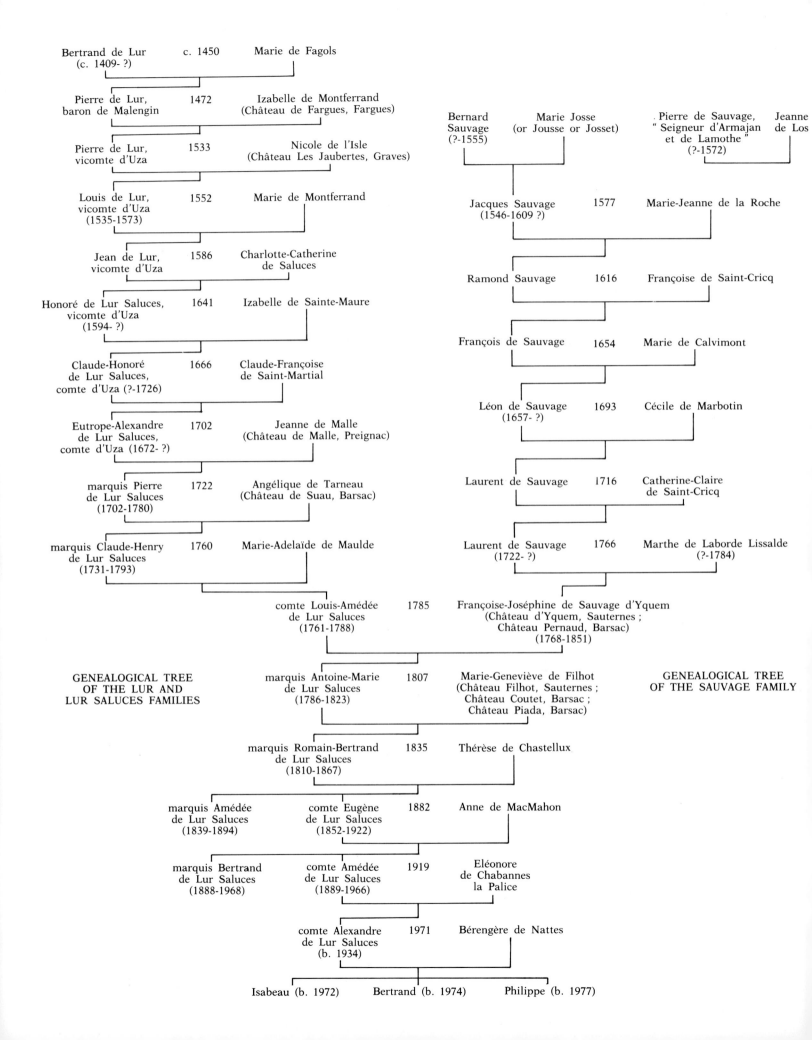

Bertrand de Lur   c. 1450   Marie de Fagols
(c. 1409- ?)

Pierre de Lur,   1472   Izabelle de Montferrand
baron de Malengin   (Château de Fargues, Fargues)

Pierre de Lur,   1533   Nicole de l'Isle
vicomte d'Uza   (Château Les Jaubertes, Graves)

Louis de Lur,   1552   Marie de Montferrand
vicomte d'Uza
(1535-1573)

Jean de Lur,   1586   Charlotte-Catherine
vicomte d'Uza   de Saluces

Honoré de Lur Saluces,   1641   Izabelle de Sainte-Maure
vicomte d'Uza
(1594- ?)

Claude-Honoré   1666   Claude-Françoise
de Lur Saluces,   de Saint-Martial
comte d'Uza (?-1726)

Eutrope-Alexandre   1702   Jeanne de Malle
de Lur Saluces,   (Château de Malle, Preignac)
comte d'Uza (1672- ?)

marquis Pierre   1722   Angélique de Tarneau
de Lur Saluces   (Château de Suau, Barsac)
(1702-1780)

marquis Claude-Henry   1760   Marie-Adelaïde de Maulde
de Lur Saluces
(1731-1793)

**GENEALOGICAL TREE
OF THE LUR AND
LUR SALUCES FAMILIES**

Bernard   Marie Josse   Pierre de Sauvage,   Jeanne
Sauvage   (or Jousse or Josset)   " Seigneur d'Armajan   de Los
(?-1555)   et de Lamothe "
      (?-1572)

Jacques Sauvage   1577   Marie-Jeanne de la Roche
(1546-1609 ?)

Ramond Sauvage   1616   Françoise de Saint-Cricq

François de Sauvage   1654   Marie de Calvimont

Léon de Sauvage   1693   Cécile de Marbotin
(1657- ?)

Laurent de Sauvage   1716   Catherine-Claire
      de Saint-Cricq

Laurent de Sauvage   1766   Marthe de Laborde Lissalde
(1722- ?)   (?-1784)

comte Louis-Amédée   1785   Françoise-Joséphine de Sauvage d'Yquem
de Lur Saluces   (Château d'Yquem, Sauternes ;
(1761-1788)   Château Pernaud, Barsac)
      (1768-1851)

marquis Antoine-Marie   1807   Marie-Geneviève de Filhot
de Lur Saluces   (Château Filhot, Sauternes ;
(1786-1823)   Château Coutet, Barsac ;
      Château Piada, Barsac)

**GENEALOGICAL TREE
OF THE SAUVAGE FAMILY**

marquis Romain-Bertrand   1835   Thérèse de Chastellux
de Lur Saluces
(1810-1867)

marquis Amédée   comte Eugène   1882   Anne de MacMahon
de Lur Saluces   de Lur Saluces
(1839-1894)   (1852-1922)

marquis Bertrand   comte Amédée   1919   Eléonore
de Lur Saluces   de Lur Saluces   de Chabannes
(1888-1968)   (1889-1966)   la Palice

comte Alexandre   1971   Bérengère de Nattes
de Lur Saluces
(b. 1934)

Isabeau (b. 1972)   Bertrand (b. 1974)   Philippe (b. 1977)

1922, Filhot in 1935). Her grandson, Romain-Bertrand, was the first **Lur Saluces** to be intimately involved in the affairs of Yquem; at his death in 1867, they passed into the hands of his eldest son, the marquis Amédée de Lur Saluces, who had no descendants. His younger brother, Eugène, had two sons, Bertrand and Amédée.

The marquis Bertrand de Lur Saluces steered Yquem through two world wars and the economic crisis of the 1930s with an *élan* for which he became famous. Known in the Bordelais and in the wine world simply as "le marquis", he was one of the *monstres sacrés* of the twentieth century viticultural theatre. He was also one of the earliest crusaders for the obligatory estate bottling of the Bordeaux first growths (a concept which was anathema to the Bordeaux marketplace), a means not only of loosening the vice in which the growers had for so long been screwed by the trade, but of guaranteeing, to the mutual profit of proprietors and clients, the authenticity of a bottle's contents. President of L'Union des Crus Classés de la Gironde from its creation in 1927 until he succumbed to a heart attack in December 1968, the marquis more than once rubbed the fur of the Bordeaux *négociants* the wrong way. At his death, comte Amédée's son, comte Alexandre de Lur Saluces, assumed command at Yquem.

The Sauternes district is suffused with the Lur Saluces aura. At the entrance to the church in the village of Sauternes, a massive slab of marble, over which members of the congregation occasionally trip, marks the graves of comte Louis-Amédée's sisters, Eugénie (died 1848) and Anne-Félicité (died 1794), "les chanoinesses-comtesses de Lur Saluces". It is poetic justice that, today, Alexandre de Lur Saluces should be mayor of this peaceful

M*arquis Bertrand de Lur Saluces*
reigned over Yquem for more than half a century
until his death in 1968.

village in whose public square, not even two centuries ago, his ancestors' feudal titles were burned. Alexandre's urbane and gentle manner cannot disguise the crusading spirit and the dedication to an ideal which he has inherited from his uncle. He is an indefatigable, international ambassador-at-large, not only for Château d'Yquem but for the wines and the traditions of Sauternes, explaining and analysing Sauternes and the role of noble rot while, at the same time, defending the public image of Yquem, in and out of the law courts, against the desecrating efforts of cigar barons and other commercial parasites[6].

Alexandre de Lur Saluces is acquainted with Yquem lovers the world over, a fair number of them being in the United States. The American taste for Yquem originated with Thomas Jefferson. It was in December, 1787, that Jefferson, at that time ambassador to Versailles and future president of the newly created United States of America, wrote to John Bondfield, the American consul in Bordeaux : " Having in the course of my journey the last spring examined into the details relative to the most celebrated wines of France, and decided within my own mind which of them I would wish to have always for my own use, I have established correspondences directly with the owners of the best vineyards. It remains for me to do this at Sauterne. I have therefore written the inclosed letter to M. Diquem[7] who makes the best of that name, to begin a correspondence on this object, and to ask of him for the present 250 bottles of Sauterne of the vintage of 1784 ... I must ask you also to add on the letter the address of M. Diquem with which I am unacquainted, and to inform me of it for my future government. Perhaps I should have addressed myself to Monsr. Salus his son in Law, as I am not certain whether he is not either jointly or solely interested at present in the vineyards. " Bondfield replied that regarding the " letter to M. D'Yquem, that estate at present belongs to the Comte de Lur his son in Law to whom I inclosed your letter ... ".

A year later Jefferson writes to Bondfield : " This [Yquem] proves a most excellent wine, and seems to have hit the palate of the Americans more than any wine I have ever seen in France ". In a letter dated " Philadelphie ce 6me. 7bre. 1790 " and addressed to comte Louis-Amédée de Lur Saluces, of whose death two years earlier Jefferson is unaware, he writes, " The white wine of Sauterne, of your growth, that you were so good as to send me in Paris at the beginning of the year 1788, was so well received by the Americans who tasted it that I do not doubt that it will conform generally to the taste of my compatriots. Now that I am established here, I have persuaded our President, General Washington, to try a sample. He asks for thirty dozen [bottles], sir, and I ask you for ten dozen for myself ... ". The reply to this letter came from the comtesse Françoise-Joséphine.

Elsewhere Jefferson writes : " The [white] wines made in the canton of Grave are most esteemed at Bordeaux ... But the white wines made in the three parishes above Grave are more esteemed at Paris than the vins de Grave. These are 1. Sauterne, the best of all, belonging to M. de Lur-Saluces (who supplies me) ... 2. Prignac ... 3. Barsac ... In all cases the owner is the person to be applied to. He will either send you none, or good. He never adulterates because he would be a felo de se to do it ". In the same vein, in a letter accompanying hampers of wines to be tasted by John Jay, Secretary for Foreign Affairs, and President Washington, he writes : " The vigneron never adulterates his

Comte Alexandre de Lur Saluces.

wine, but on the contrary gives it the most perfect and pure [care] possible. But when once a wine has been into a merchant's hands, it never comes out unmixed. This being the basis of their trade, no degree of honesty, of personal friendship or of kindred prevents it." More than a century and a half before "la mise en bouteilles au château" became generalized, Jefferson insisted that his wines be put into bottles by the proprietors themselves. And vintages were taken very seriously: Jefferson noted in 1787 that "The best vintage now to be bought is of 1784 ... there has been no other good year since 1779"[8]. This was perhaps an exaggeration – 1784 was no doubt an unusual vintage but 1783, 1785 and 1786 are known to have produced good wines. As for 1787, the wine was found to be powerful, luscious and harmonious, tasted two centuries later, in the month of May 1985, at Yquem.

Thus, in broad brush strokes, is the history of Yquem and of the families that preside and have presided over its destinies, a history whose examination in detail is at its mere beginnings and which remains to be unveiled from amongst the archives harboured in one of the château's towers. Here lies an incredible store of documents – crates, cartons, bundles, ledgers, files, shelved or stacked on all sides from floor to ceiling, a vast table piled high in the middle of the room – which has accumulated over the last couple of centuries. Philippe Roudié, professor at the University of Bordeaux, who has accepted the task of classifying and analysing this storehouse, is categorical in his assertion that these are by far the most extensive records relating to any of the great Bordeaux domains... And his eyes glisten with excitement at the mere sight of this intimidating mountain of dusty documents. No doubt, the definitive work on Château d'Yquem will one day be signed "Philippe Roudié" – a long and arduous task it will be, for even the few documents examined thus far reveal an incredible profusion of information.

*The comte and the comtesse
Alexandre de Lur Saluces with their children,
(left to right) Philippe, Bertrand and Isabeau.*

26

CHATEAU D' YQUEM TODAY

Visitors to Yquem are often overcome by a dream-like sense of moving out of time – not so much moving back in time, as some suggest, but rather a vague sense of timelessness, of touching something that is eternal. The silence contributes hugely for we have become unaccustomed to the absence of city and motorway sounds. The undulating panorama of vines, punctuated by reaches of wooded areas that obscure all roadways, stretching in all directions to the horizon, and the friendly contours of the château are cloaked in this silence of which the air and the light are also part.

This extraordinary sense of well-being may, momentarily, lull one into envisaging Yquem as a sort of bucolic anachronism. The two remaining work horses, *Popaul* and *Pompon*, do their best to reinforce this impression but, in fact, they are kept mainly for their comforting presence, to pose for photographers and, above all, for the humane purpose of occupying a couple of artisans moulded in the subtle art of guiding horses with a secret language constructed of imperceptible movements, clucks and whispers. An impressive stable of *enjambeurs*, the high-perched tractors especially invented to straddle rows of vines, has long since replaced oxen, horses and, in some instances, *vignerons*, in the vineyard. In so far as nature permits, Yquem is a highly organized and well-oiled machine.

At present, the property covers 173 hectares (427 acres)[9], 102 hectares (252 acres) of which are vineyard ; meadows and pine woods occupy the remainder. About 90 hectares (220 acres) are in production at a given time, the rest of the vineyard lying fallow for a period after the uprooting of old vines or being given over to young plantations not yet in production.

Château d'Yquem, from which the vines slope down on all sides, occupies the highest point in the Sauternes region. A patchwork structure of loopholed round towers, square towers, crenellated walls, simple farmhouse architecture and seigneurial castle, enclosing a large square courtyard with gates opening to the south-east and to the north-west and, at its heart, a massive well wound round with climbing roses. None the less, the disparate

Winter view of the château d'Yquem and
its cellars before the vines have been pruned (following pages).

structures form a remarkable whole, fusing in perfect harmony with the space of the courtyard, beautiful and moving in its human dimensions and total absence of pomp. The round towers, their medieval allure notwithstanding, are fifteenth century. The well is sixteenth century and the remainder of the architecture dates from the sixteenth and seventeenth centuries.

To the left of the south-east entrance to the courtyard spreads a typically majestic cedar of Lebanon whose bearing suggests a presence of many centuries (belied by photographs from the last century showing no cedar); in the autumn, wild cyclamens are

scattered thickly beneath it, a fantastic carpet of lavender, lilac and violet tones, accented with strokes of white.

Although uninhabited, the château is well kept up and the comte and the comtesse often receive visitors there, simply or magnificently depending on the circumstances. A bank of camelias lines one of the outside walls of the château and other unscented flowers are cultivated in the gardens from which to create the dining table's floral centrepieces, always of a singular beauty, while never threatening to trouble an Yquem's bouquet.

The menu may be composed of dishes specially conceived to throw into relief a gamut of vintages of Château de Fargues (another Sauternes property belonging to the Lur Saluces) and of Yquem, or it may be a comfortable family meal with a claret placed

Aerial view of the château and the estate.

between two Sauternes. One of Bordeaux's celebrated restaurateurs often caters for the more elaborate meals ; on other occasions, one of the staff, a woman who can roast a leg of lamb or grill an entrecôte to perfection while tossing the cèpes à la bordelaise, is in the kitchen. Guy Latrille, the cellar-master, and his assistant are in charge of the wine service at formal meals. At more intimate gatherings, Thérèse, one of the estate's vineyard workers, who also looks after the château, pours the wine, always at a perfect temperature, with discretion, style and a quiet pride in her role.

Each month of May, the courtyard, already at its most resplendent with the rose bushes and climbers in full flower, is decked out in fancy dress, in preparation for a gala fête featuring a chamber music concert, one of the cornerstones of the annual Bordeaux festival, " Le Mai Musical ". A reception in the château follows the concert, a sparkling soirée at which, crowning the surrounding countryside, Yquem's medieval contours may be seen bathed in an irreal play of spotlights.

Alexandre de Lur Saluces's righthand is Pierre Meslier, *régisseur*, or director, since 1963 of both Château d'Yquem and Château de Fargues (165 hectares, mostly pines and meadows, 13 hectares of which are planted to vines from which a perfect Sauternes, less exalted than Yquem, is extracted). To his remarkable qualities as *régisseur* are joined the degree of agricultural engineer and the talents of impassioned *vigneron*, dishevelled poet and brilliant exponent of the wines of Sauternes and the mysteries of *pourriture noble*, or noble rot, the magical mycoflora that alters the grape's structure, conferring upon the wine its golden cloak and its pulsating, liquorous vitality.

The other key figure is Guy Latrille, *maître de chais*, cellar-master, who nurses the vintage from the time that the grapes arrive at the *chai* until the moment the wine is bottled three and a half years later. In the words of Alexandre de Lur Saluces, " It is Guy Latrille who commands Pierre Meslier and it is Pierre Meslier who commands me. "

Forty-eight *vignerons* live and work at Yquem, forming a semi-self-sufficient agricultural community that shares a certain interdependence with its sister community at Château de Fargues. The concept is based on a traditional Bordeaux system known as *prix-fait*, by which each family was housed and received certain benefits plus a fixed salary in exchange for the year-round care, except for picking, of a precisely defined area of vines, any extra work incurred outside this area being paid for on a time basis.

They are still housed as before, they receive the same benefits, and each person has a fixed salary. But the technology of modern viticulture has imposed a completely different structure on the work pattern. Of the traditional mens' chores, deep and shallow ploughing, hoeing, treating the vines against maladies and pests, and *rognage*, or summer pruning, are all mechanized today. Only winter pruning, the replacement and upkeep of the *piquets d'acacia*, or locust-wood stakes, in the vine rows and the tightening of the wires that are attached to them must still be done by hand. The women's work – gathering and bundling or burning the pruned wood, attaching the vine branches to wires, removing unwanted shoots in the spring, autumn defoliation – is still done by hand. Pierre Meslier figures that, whereas about 70 per cent of the women's work is still done on a *prix-fait* basis, only 30 per cent of the men's work is now on *prix-fait*, the remainder being paid on a time basis.

31

Partly because of mechanization, and partly because now everyone works on a full-time basis there are fewer workers than in the past; both the *prix-fait* salaries and the wage earnings are established in terms of the individual's capabilities. The total number of personnel is based on the number of men needed for winter pruning, the most crucial and exacting of the *prix-fait* chores. Using the different talents available, there is no problem in keeping everyone busy on a time-paid basis to fill in the year: apart from tractor work in the vineyard, there is planting and grafting to be done, there are carpentry, blacksmith and mechanics workshops on the property, and masons are needed. During the harvest everyone picks and up to eighty experienced pickers must be brought in from the neighbouring countryside and villages to supplement the regular estate workers.

The sense of insularity, the feeling that the Yquem "family" is a race apart and that, at Yquem, things are not done in quite the same way as elsewhere is marked. Many of the workers were born at Yquem and some families have been there for several generations. Each family has a house with a garden for growing vegetables and space in which to keep a few chickens, rabbits and a couple of pigs. Each *vigneron* receives a monthly ration of a quarter of a cask (56 litres) of red wine, in accordance with " les usages loyaux et constants " (" faithful and steadfast customs "); to provide this 3 hectares (7 acres) of Cabernet and Merlot vines are planted at the southern extreme of the property and their grapes are vinified in a small modern *chai* in the workyard.

A typical country grocery co-operative, operated by the estate workers, is installed in one of the rooms of the château opening onto the courtyard – sausages hang from an overhead beam while basic foods and canned goods intermingle with piles of felt slippers, rubber boots and sacks of chicken-feed. In principle, it is only open on Fridays but, in fact, it will open at any time if an Yquem villager needs something. A baker visits Yquem daily and a butcher's van alternates visits with a fishmonger's van at given hours on specified days.

Château d'Yquem is born from the unhindered collaboration of natural circumstances. Man's contributions are aimed at creating, directing or safeguarding a biological arena in which nature's gifts can most perfectly carry out their transformations.

Yquem owes its exceptional success, first of all, to the soil – the most mysterious of all the quality factors –; to its situation in the most perfect of microclimates for the proliferation of *botrytis cinerea*, called noble rot; to an extensive draining system which supplements the natural drainage afforded by the stony soil and the sloping hillsides; to the age of the vines and to the care given to them to limit production. Amongst the contributory factors to these basic conditions are: the progressive genetic refinement of the vineyard's two grape varieties (80 per cent Sémillon and 20 per cent Sauvignon) by reproduction from carefully selected cuttings on the property; a special method of picking which consists in passing repeatedly through the vineyard to pluck individual grapes from the bunches; an unconditional refusal to chaptalize[10]; the exclusive use of new oak barrels for fermenting and raising the wine; and a refusal to bottle under the Yquem label any wine that does not conform to Yquem's standard of perfection.

The property's overall average annual production of wine – not all of which becomes Château d'Yquem – is about 9 hectolitres per hectare (95 gallons per acre) or the equivalent

The estate workers' grocery co-operative.

Guy Latrille, cellar master, and Pierre Meslier, régisseur, in the cellars.

Pierre Meslier, régisseur of Château d'Yquem and Château de Fargues since 1963.

of a single glass of wine per vine, without doubt the smallest quantity of wine from a given area of vines of any rationally operated vineyard in the world. But, for such a figure to be meaningful, a number of other figures must be brought into play[11]. In an extraordinarily bountiful vintage, for instance, a production of from 12 to 13 hectolitres per hectare (128 to 138 gallons per acre) is possible; in equally unusual years, hail (1952) or rain (1964) may destroy the entire harvest, or poor weather may reduce it pitifully.

The average and the maximum figures represent the overall quantity of wine produced, and not that which is bottled under the label of Château d'Yquem; a rigid selection always eliminates a certain number of barrels which are then sold to the trade as generic Sauternes with no indication of its origin. On an average of once each decade, there is no Château d'Yquem (1930, 1951, 1952, 1964, 1972, 1974 ...). In recent years, the following proportions of the vintage have been retained for Château d'Yquem bottlings:

1983 : 80 %	1978 : 15 %	1973 : 12 %	1968 : 10 %
1982 : 33 %	1977 : 30 %	1972 : 0 %	1967 : 90 %
1981 : 80 %	1976 : 90 %	1971 : 80 %	1966 : 80 %
1980 : 80 %	1975 : 80 %	1970 : 80 %	1965 : 50 %
1979 : 40 %	1974 : 0 %	1969 : 60 %	1964 : 0 %

With an uncontrolled distribution, such an erratic production would inevitably empty the coffers in lean years – and, in the past, has been known to do so. Thus an astute formula of commercialization, destined to adapt itself to the caprices of nature and to relax the squeeze of difficult years, has been established. The total number of bottles of Château d'Yquem produced over a twenty-year period has been reduced to the mean annual figure of 66,000 (see note 9). This, by comparison with the total production figures given above, means that the average production of wine that is bottled under Château d'Yquem labels is just over 6 hectolitres per hectare, or 65 gallons per acre. Unlike the prestigious red growths from the other Bordeaux regions, whose wines (in good years) are all sold while still in the wood, to be delivered after bottling – a system which encourages speculation in the trade, usually at the grower's expense – Yquem is never sold until after it is bottled and, then, it is released in relatively small lots at a time. Two, sometimes three, times each year the decision is made to release a certain number of bottles of one or more vintages. Then, two Bordeaux *courtier* firms are called in; *courtiers* or wine brokers, are official mediators, permitting growers and *négociants*, or shippers, to agree on prices and conditions of payment, dates of delivery and the quantity as well as the apportionment of the wine to be released. This service is equally precious to the shipper, who need not leave his offices, and to the proprietor who does not, in Alexandre de Lur Saluces's case, have to call upon the nine different Bordeaux shippers, the traditional recipients of Yquem. And it allows everyone to remain on good terms despite the difficulties of adjusting offer and demand.

Too many unforeseen circumstances can induce a tightening or loosening of the reins to permit identical annual releases; in reality, the number of bottles released each year falls within a range of 63,000 to 70,000. The choice of vintages and the number of bottles released every few months relates to an eight-year span of vintages, some still in casks and others in bottles, awaiting a propitious date for release. The relative abundance of recent vintages, the ageing propensities of different vintages, the economic climate, and the often stubborn prejudices of the market-place all exert their influences.

What a *négociant* is willing to pay for a wine relates less to the quality or future of the wine than to the immediate public demand, which is always coloured by the generalized reputation of a vintage. Thus Sauternes is often a vintage-chart victim, the reputation of

a red Bordeaux vintage shedding a false light on the luscious white wines. For example, 1967 produced an abundance of red Bordeaux, said to be for rapid drinking and considered by the trade to be a useful, " honestly priced ", run-of-the-mill vintage. At Yquem, with the 1967, they knew that they had a giant on their hands but, in 1971 when it was bottled, the trade preferred to treat it as an " off vintage ", offering 1967 red wine prices. Yquem's policy of holding stock and portioning distribution permitted them to shelve the 1967 until the trade was able to recognize its value ; there were still '65s and '66s to be released before the '68s and the '69s took over the relay. A few years later, the once reticent buyers were beginning to realize that 1967 had already joined the roster of Yquem's mythical vintages.

Professor Philippe Roudié at work in Yquem's archives.

The elaboration of what, finally, can only be defined as a work of art, welded out of nature's uncertain beneficence, tempered by tradition and Draconian principles, is a precarious *métier* and the makers of Yquem walk a perpetual tight-rope. One need not check the accounting ledgers to be certain that the immense profit that Alexandre de Lur Saluces derives from Château d'Yquem resides mainly in the personal pride and satisfaction of being able to permit this uncommon wine, untainted by compromise, to exist.

This skeletal outline demands a lot of fleshing out to explain what makes Château d'Yquem what it is – and the explanations are not always simple, nor are the answers to the questions always the same. Alexandre de Lur Saluces recalls having received a distinguished group of international management consultants at Yquem. Their questions were pointed and penetrating. Both he and his interrogators became increasingly uncomfortable as he responded to question after question with, " Well, that depends ... ". It was his impression that his guests were uncertain as to whether he was rather awkwardly attempting to veil malodorous viticultural practices or whether, in fact, he was unable, himself, to grasp the complexities of the miraculous thing with which his name is so intimately associated. Apologizing for his inadequacy, he decided to solicit the talents of Pierre Meslier, whose lucid and detailed explanations have enlightened thousands of visitors to Yquem over the last twenty years. In response to the first question, Mr Meslier paused, mulled it over, and murmured, " Well, that depends ... ".

Accounting ledgers from the archives.

NOBLE ROT

Luscious wine was the term commonly used in the last century to describe a naturally vinified wine which retained a high degree of unfermented grape sugars. It is a pity that it has fallen out of use, for its present substitutes, "sweet wine" or "dessert wine", carry too many unfortunate associations to be acceptable definitions of Sauternes.

It is possible to make a luscious wine from partially dried grapes whose sugars, acids and other components are physically concentrated by desiccation but are chemically unaltered, the fermentation of the musts being arrested as the rising alcohol level paralyses the yeasts, leaving a certain amount of unfermented sugar in the wine. Such are the traditional *vins de paille* and such were the wines whose vinification was described by Hesiod nearly 3000 years ago. But, for the elaboration of the most sublime of luscious wines, a phenomenon far more complex than that of simple desiccation is crucial. This phenomenon begins with the progressive invasion of a vineyard by a parasitic fungus, insidious and repellent in appearance to the uninitiated, whose scientific name, a hybrid of Greek and Latin, is *botrytis cinerea* and means "ashen bunch of grapes". It is commonly known as *pourriture noble* or noble rot, and familiarly, to the Sauternes *vigneron*, simply as *la pourriture*. As it forms on the individual grapes, spreading irregularly from one to another on a single bunch, from one bunch to another, and from one part of the vineyard to another, its root-like filaments, or mycelium, penetrate the skins of the ripe grapes, mortifying them while maintaining them intact, leaving no path of entrance for less beneficent microbial life, while the noble rot feeds itself on the grape's sugars and acids. Each full, ripe, tight-skinned yellow grape is first lightly scattered with brown, pin-

An early picking (left-hand page).

point speckles, the skin then veers towards dull pinks and violets, turning progressively browner before the grape begins to shrink, a powdery, ashen mould sometimes forming on its rumpled surface. For ease of communication, the infinite number of stages in this transformation are divided into three categories : 1. *grains verts* (" green " grapes), the fully ripened but unaltered grapes ; 2. *grains pourris pleins* (rotted full grapes), grapes that have been affected by the fungus but are still plump, juicy and smooth-surfaced – the skins have turned brown but dehydration has not yet set in ; 3. *grains rôtis* (roasted grapes), dried and withered grapes, often covered with the fungus bloom.

This progression of visual alterations is the outward signal of a frenzy of chemical activity and structural changes within each grape. While consuming about one-third of the grapes' sugars, the fungus feeds ravenously on the tartaric acid, the principal acid contained in grapes, diminishing it by some five-sixths of the original amount ; the malic acid, whose presence in a normally ripened grape is slight by comparison with that of the tartaric acid, is diminished by about one-third ; and the minimal traces of citric acid by about one-quarter. The noble rot also uses up much of the grapes' water while, at the same time, its disintegrating action on the skins renders them extremely porous and facilitates an additional loss of water through evaporation from the effects of sun and wind ; the diminution of weight due to loss of water and to combustion varies from half to two-thirds.

An elusive antibiotic substance which has been given the name of " botryticine " is manufactured in the course of this selective digestive process, as well as other new elements – glycerol, gluconic acid, dextrin – which give the wine its voluptuous texture or unctuousness. Meanwhile, the molecular structure of the grapes' skins has been broken down by the action of the *botrytis cinerea*, much in the same way as, in the vinification of red wine where the crushed mass of grapes is fermented on the skins, the alcohol breaks down the molecular structure of the skins, destroying their resistance and freeing not only the colour but the tannins which, in white wines made from normally ripened grapes, remain almost entirely imprisoned in the resistant skins of the pressed grapes. When grapes affected by noble rot are pressed, the tannins are released into the juice.

The overall effect of these various physical and chemical alterations is that of a general deacidification, an intense concentration of the natural grape sugars and a sharply heightened tannic presence in a radically reduced quantity of must, in combination with a number of newly manufactured elements – in short, a completely new chemical and physical structure or fermenting medium. The important message to be gleaned from this simplified explanation of a complex transformation is that a new taste is born – a magical taste unlike that of any other wine.

When *botrytis cinerea* attacks grapes that have not completely ripened or have been punctured, split or otherwise damaged by birds, rain or hail, wasps or other insects, it is called *pourriture grise* or grey rot, and counts amongst the most destructive of the *vigneron's* enemies. It deepens the wounds in the grapes, clearing a path for the traffic of harmful bacteria ; the contact with air launches a beginning of alcoholic fermentation and, simultaneously, of acetic fermentation and decay ; where red grapes are concerned, the botrytis destroys the pigmentation in the skins.

Bunch of grapes before complete ripening (1).
(2) Slight discolouration indicates the beginnings of botrytis.
(3) A bunch of Sémillon grapes at the moment of the first trie with intermixture of
grains verts, grains pourris-pleins and grains rôtis.
(4) Grains rôtis.

41

For this perverse cryptogam to operate in its noble phase, a number of specific circumstances are essential : the grape varieties should be white, early-ripening and endowed with relatively thick skins that will resist splitting from the disintegrating action of the rot ; the grapes should be healthy, whole and fully ripened before the fungus manifests itself ; the regional climate should be temperate ; a combination of the geographical situation and the autumn weather should provide early morning mists followed by clear, warm and sunny days (hillsides in river valleys are classic sites). A gentle and progressive invasion of botrytis is best controlled by the alternating factors of morning humidity to encourage it and the healthy, drying effects of the sun to restrain too rapid a development. If the weather becomes overcast and humid or rainy, even healthy, ripe grapes may be subjected to a botrytis invasion so intense that the skins cannot resist the attack, then they will split and noble beginnings will collapse into dread grey rot. On the other hand, in a prolonged, hot autumn with insufficient morning humidity, the fungus may never appear or it may be destroyed at inception by the dry heat and the grapes will eventually wither, concentrating their various constituents, to produce a wine like that described at the beginning of the chapter.

Finally, under certain circumstances, the absence of the hoped-for alternations of morning mists and sunny days need not be a disaster. If the grapes have ripened under healthy conditions, the onset of rainy weather following physiological maturity may still permit a normal development of noble rot, with low temperatures preventing its dissolution into grey rot while the withering action of late autumnal winds dries out the grapes to achieve the necessary sugar concentration. The salutary effects of a November east wind were largely responsible for the success of both the 1980 and the 1981 vintages at Yquem.

Botrytis, of course, is not bound to only two modes of activity, one totally good and the other totally bad. It is certain that damaged grapes, under any weather conditions, will never rot nobly. Given perfectly healthy, ripe grapes, however, weather variations within a generally favourable range will incite different degrees of perfection in the noble rot's performance. The dusty mould which usually forms on the surface of the wrinkling grapes and which rises in a smoky cloud when they are tumbled from one recipient to another is, in fact, a manifestation of grey rot but, as long as the skins remain intact, barring entrance to harmful bacteria, its action is benign. Transcendent noble rot, usually following a hot summer and early ripening with continuing dry autumn heat and a modicum of early morning humidity, is expressed by the same transformations of skin and pulp and by the same withering desiccation but without the aerial development of the mushroom in the form of surface mould.

Some aspects of the fungus's activity remain mysterious : œnologists figure that, in a particularly favoured microclimate like that of Sauternes, colonies of closely related strains, especially adapted to the parasite's noble function and less apt to cause pernicious grey rot, must establish themselves in the vineyards, much in the same way that, over a long period of time, a natural selection of yeasts will colonize vineyards and cellars, helping to define the personality of a specific wine.

To profit fully from the effects of noble rot, each individual grape should be picked at a particular stage of development. As the fungus begins to spread, each bunch of grapes

A *late* trie *of* grains rôtis.

will present individual grapes, alone or in small clusters, at varying stages of development. Because the invasion is usually irregular and often slow, both within the entire vineyard and within each bunch of grapes, and because those that have arrived at the *rôti* stage must not be permitted to shrink further, the pickers pass repeatedly through the vineyard, removing from each bunch of grapes only the individual grapes or small clusters of grapes that have shrivelled to the desired degree. These selective pickings are called *tries*. It is an unusual vintage that permits all the grapes to be picked in four *tries* or in less than a month's time; eight to ten *tries* over the space of two months or more are not uncommon.

In the fifth century BC the Greeks drank a wine called *saprian*. In *The Deipnosophists*, Atheneus, the second century AD Greek-Egyptian historian-gastronomer, quotes a line from a lost play by Hermippus in which Dionysus, after giving the wine of Chios particularly high praise, says, " But there is a wine which they call saprian and from the mouths of the jars as they are opened rises the scent of violets, the scent of roses, the scent of hyacinth. A divine fragrance fills the vast house, ambrosia and nectar in one." It is not clear here whether *saprian* is one of the wines of Chios but, in another passage a citation, also from the fifth century AD, describes Chian wine as *sapros*.

The literal translation of *sapros* is " rotten, putrid, diseased, decayed...". Translators, who give it this meaning in all contexts except that of wine, are apparently puzzled at the sobriquet, " rotten ", when applied to a wine possessed of a fresh floral bouquet and obviously considered to be of great finesse. An eighteenth century French translation leaves the word in the original Greek with no attempt at explanation; a recent translator tentatively suggests *vin bléti* (overripe wine) as a translation for *saprian*, with the observation that it is an astonishing word choice to describe a wine favourably; the English translator settles for " mellow " with no comment.

For no apparent reason writers have always assumed *saprian* to have been a red wine. To support this theory, comte Odart, in his *Ampélographie universelle* (1874), incorrectly identifies *saprian* with pramnian wine, described elsewhere in *The Deipnosophists* as " neither sweet nor rich but dry, hard and of extraordinary strength ... [pramnian wines] contract the eyebrows as well as the bowels ". " Saprias ", he says, " is synonymous with rancio [rancid] ", a term applied today to certain fortified red wines with a typically oxidized flavour. The English writer, Warner Allen, likens Hermippus's floral description to a Château Margaux 1871 and then rather lamely calls to witness high game and ripe cheese to justify the use of " rotten " in a positive sense; by circumlocutory means, quoting Horace's use of the word, *rancidus* to describe high boar, he, too, settles on *rancio* as the proper equivalent to *sapros*.

It is mere conjecture, but it seems very natural that the ancient Greek *vigneron*, deliberately awaiting the moment when his plump, ripe grapes turned withered and grey before picking them, should so christen his wine in recognition of this miraculous rot that bestowed upon it the cloak of divinity. Similarly, the Sauternes *vigneron* speaks familiarly of *la pourriture*, while those of us who are less intimately bound to the vine prefer either to modify the reality by ennobling it, or to mask it with the epithet *surmaturation* which means overripe.

Noble rot (left-hand page).

If the above thesis is correct, the tradition of vinifying nobly rotted grapes had, none the less, dissipated long before Atheneus quoted the poets of Greece's golden age six centuries later. Some two thousand years appear to have then passed before the ancient methods were either reborn or thought worthy of mention, for the deliberate exploitation of noble rot in the modern world cannot be detected in historical documents earlier than the seventeenth century. (This is not too surprising for, in the preceding centuries, records concerning wine are almost entirely commercial, mentioning regions of origin, prices, taxes, and so on, the only occasional descriptive precision being the colour.)

Legends concerning accidentally retarded harvests and the subsequent discovery of a wondrous wine made from shrivelled and unsavoury-looking grapes place the first vintage of this kind in the Tokay vineyards in 1650 and in the vineyards of the Rheingau in 1775.

A flimsy legend – but one, at least until very recently, generally subscribed to – places the discovery of noble rot in Sauternes, specifically at Château d'Yquem, as late as 1847 (the same vintage whose legend was further glorified when, twelve years later, the Grand Duke Constantine, brother to the tsar of Russia, paid 20,000 francs for a 900-litre tun, approximately four times the price paid for a wine in France until then). The marquis Romain-Bertrand de Lur Saluces is said to have left instructions not to harvest the grapes until his return from a hunting trip to Russia ; the voyage was prolonged and, arriving at Yquem late in the season, the entire vineyard was found to be contaminated with noble rot. It is a curious anecdote for, not only are there a number of earlier historical references to repeated *tries* or to late harvests, but it is unlikely that the authoritative presence at Yquem of Romain-Bertrand's grandmother, the redoubtable comtesse Joséphine, née Sauvage, would have tolerated any such nonsense as an unintentionally retarded harvest. Only the transcendental quality of the vintage itself can have been responsible for the subsequent weaving of the legend.

Eventually the Yquem archives will surely reveal more detailed information. Meanwhile, one page from the cellar book, covering the month of October, 1810, provides sufficient proof that late harvests and selective pickings were already established tradition at the beginning of the nineteenth century. Picking began on 3 October and finished on 3 November with three *tries* : the first two were brief, the second lasting from 9 October to 11 October, then a pause of nine days, followed by fifteen days of continuous picking ; the 20 October entry reads : " Commencer à vendanger pour la troisième fois... " (" Begin picking for the third time ... ").

Upon reading Bidet (*Traité sur la nature et sur la culture de la vigne,* 1759), there remains no doubt that, in the mid-eighteenth century, not only were the wines of Sauternes *doux et liquoreux* (sweet and luscious) but that these were also the qualities aimed for by makers of white wine in less-privileged regions. Of the wine of the Entre-Deux-Mers, he writes, " ... one always tries, in so far as possible, to make it by resuming picking several times over, and by cutting only those grapes that are extremely ripe. In certain years, the favours of the seasons procure this success ; but it is quite rare ". And, of the wines known today as Sauternes, he writes : " ... amongst the sweet wines are no doubt those of Barsac, Preignac, Langon : their sweetness has this in particular, that not only is it mingled with much strength or spirit ; but that this sweetness sustains the wine and augments the longer one keeps it. These are not *vins de primeur*, that is to say, they are not sold early in the season, whether because the grapes are picked late or because the wines improve in the cellars and augment in price with age. Kept for twenty or thirty years, they become equal or superior to the wines of Spain, the Canaries and Malaga, and they are called *vins de l'arrière-saison* ...".

But for the wines chosen for the sake of comparison, this is a very acceptable description of today's Sauternes.

Most interesting, however, is a wisp of information from a deed, dated 4 October 1666 and drawn up by "Fontanieu, notaire à Barsac" as a result of a litigation between François de Sauvage, "sieur Diquem", and several of his tenants who wanted to pick too early. The deed states categorically, " Il n'est cousteume de vendanger annuellement en Bousmes et Sauternes que vers le quinziesme d'octobre " (" It is not customary in Bommes and Sauternes to begin picking before about the fifteenth of October. ")[12].

The lateness of the date is particularly striking if one considers that, in the present century, picking has begun that late in only seven vintages (five within the last decade) and that, including vintages that produced no Yquem, it has begun in the month of October only nineteen times.

There is only one possible interpretation of this phrase : it was François de Sauvage's intention (and perhaps that of his forebears) that picking should begin only when the entire vineyard was infested with noble rot which, in most years, is a normal condition by mid-October (the formula was undoubtedly sufficiently flexible to bend to the exigencies of a precocious or tardy botrytis manifestation) ; and his purpose was to make a wine of the same luscious intensity as the Yquems of today.

With a tradition of such late picking, it is unlikely that the system of repeated *tries* would have been refined to any degree, but the obvious determination to work with a maximum of botrytis-affected harvest probably imposed a certain amount of selective picking in difficult years. Even at Yquem today, it is only in such years, rarely the greatest, that up to eleven *tries* (1974 – no Yquem) over a period of up to seventy-one days (1972 – no Yquem) are necessary. There are equally unusual years in which it could be said that selective picking is more a matter of form than of necessity. In 1976, for example, after a precursory first *trie*, the invasion of noble rot was so rapid and so widespread, the definition of the individual grapes disappearing in the fungus-softened contours of the clusters, that the entire vintage was picked the second time around, in whole bunches and in haste, to avoid reaching such a concentration of sugars as to render fermentation impossible. Under these circumstances, any remaining " green " grapes (that is, ripe but unaffected by botrytis) are a welcome antidote to an excess of sugar and of botryticine. The 1976 picking was finished by the time that François de Sauvage normally commenced his harvest ; it lasted only twenty-two days, from 21 September to 13 October (the average is about forty-five days and 15 October usually falls about midway).

There is much that will never be uncovered about vinification at Yquem in the seventeenth century but, if one assumes that the concept of successive *tries* was either non-existent or, at most, in a formative stage and that the control of the potential balance between alcohol and residual sugar lay mainly in the decision to pick grapes that were predominantly altered by noble rot, we can make a pretty good guess that some vintages were not unlike those that have made Yquem's reputation today; that, because of the more or less inhibiting effect on fermentation of different intensities of botryticine, others were either sweeter and lower in alcohol or less sweet and higher in alcohol than today's Yquems; that a vintage like 1978, unusually late and relatively unaffected by noble rot, would simply have produced a fine dry wine; and that, occasionally, as today, poor wines from a disastrous season would have to be sent off to the distillery.

Less than a century separates François de Sauvage's late harvests from Monsieur Bidet's testimony that these wines continued to improve for twenty to thirty years, their quality of sweetness augmenting. At a half-way point, towards the end of the seventeenth century, Dom Pérignon's experiments, destined to imprison the bubbles in Champagne, had opened the way to the bottling and laying down of all wines with long ageing potential. This is not to say that François de Sauvage's Yquem could not have been kept for many years in the wood – it almost certainly was, probably in *foudres*, large tuns in which the wine's evolution is much less rapid than in the traditional *barriques bordelaises*, or hogsheads – but it is easy to believe that the perfecting of bottles and corks to seal wine away from oxidizing influences eventually heightened an awareness of the other-worldly beauty that long ageing confers upon these wines, and hastened the general practice of repeated selective pickings.

In moments of economic depression, the expensive tradition of selecting pickings may have been modified or partially abandoned in the Sauternes district (though no records link Yquem to these fluctuations). This is said to have happened in 1823, the low prices obtained for their wines forcing growers to economize by picking all the grapes at once; thirteen years later a retarded harvest, imposed by difficult weather conditions, produced a luscious wine that inspired growers to reinstate the tradition. Memory is short and this gave rise to yet another legend – less widespread than the tale of the 1847 vintage – crediting 1836 with the first liquorous Sauternes and the subsequent imposition of late harvests and selective pickings.

Noble rot is a natural phenomenon and, in most years, an inevitable presence in the Sauternes vineyards, its annual beginnings normally coinciding with the physiological maturity of the grapes during the last half of September. If one brushes aside the recurrent and conflicting legends for which, in each instance, the only explanation would appear to be an innocent attempt to justify the use of " rotten " grapes to make a very special wine, it seems obvious that, in a microclimate providing the most perfect conjunction of natural conditions for its proliferation, the Sauternes *vigneron* can, at no time in the history of the vineyard, have been ignorant of the presence of noble rot or of its effects on his wine.

At *the moment of the first* trie, *a few shrunken grapes
are ready to be plucked individually from the bunches (right-hand page).*

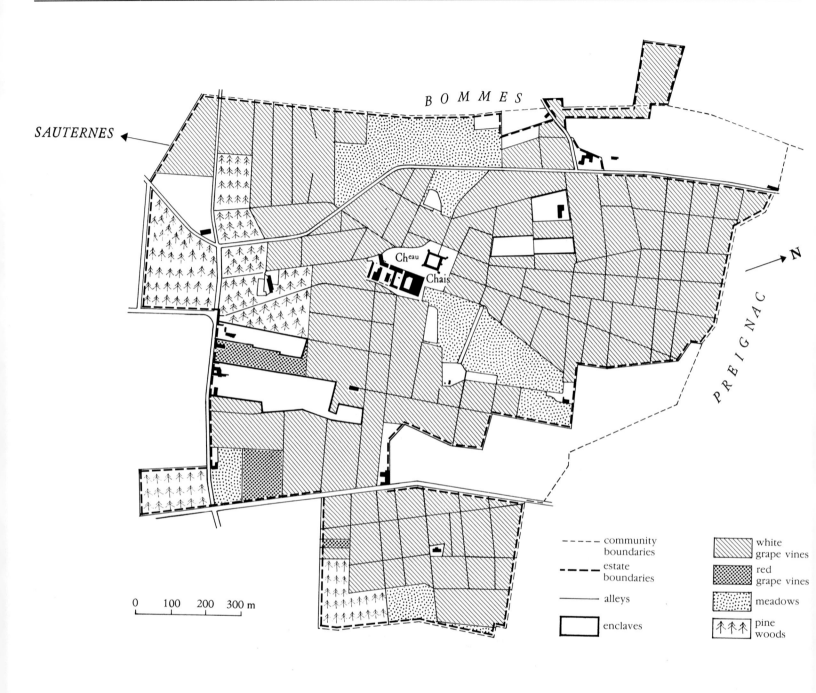

BOMMES

SAUTERNES

PREIGNAC

N

Ch^eau
Chais

- - - - - community
boundaries

———— estate
boundaries

————— alleys

enclaves

0   100   200   300 m

white
grape vines

red
grape vines

meadows

pine
woods

The estate of Yquem.

50

THE GENIUS
OF THE SOIL

Sauternes forms a small enclave within the southern tip of the Graves region, not quite fifty kilometres (thirty miles) from the city of Bordeaux. The strip of land called Graves, which takes its name from the abundance of pebbles which characterizes its soil structure, lies along the left bank of the Garonne river. With the Médoc, to the north of the city, it forms a single geographical and geological entity punctuated by the chain of undulating, gravelly mounds or *croupes*, impoverished by erosion, that were created a couple of million years ago by violent chthonic shufflings and torrential deposits (at Yquem predominantly Pyrenean) and that now situate the greatest growths of the Médoc, Graves and Sauternes. The entire region also shares a common microclimate, tempered by the proximity of the Garonne and Gironde rivers and protected from ocean winds by the solid mass of pine forests in the Landes to the west. Sauternes, cradled between the valleys of the Garonne and its small tributary, the Ciron, enjoys a microclimate within a microclimate, the vapours from the two rivers joining to cloak the vineyards in the autumnal morning mists that favour the development of noble rot.

The vines of Yquem are spread over one immense *croupe*, with the château and the vinification cellars, or *chais*, at its summit, an altitude of some 75 metres (250 ft), dominating not only the property itself but all of Sauternes; at the northern extremity of the vineyard the slope descends to an altitude of 40 metres (130 ft).

The conjunction of old vines, hillsides or slopes and a stony soil, so arid as to be useless for other crops, has always been considered of fundamental importance to the production of great wine. The poverty of the topsoil forces the vine's roots to wind a deep path through the earth's resistant substrata – a voyage that takes many years – in search of nourishment whose mineral complexity is vital to the wine's character.

51

The vineyard in summer and in winter.
Vines in autumn to the north-west of the
château (right-hand page).

Inclines are necessary to keep the soil well drained (the vines' roots must never stagnate in trapped pockets of water), and to keep it poor. In Sauternes, where the climate is gentle and the altitudes never sufficiently elevated to alter the temperature noticeably, the best wines come from the highest parts of the hillsides where the soils are the poorest.

The pebbles fulfil so many essential functions that, in the Bordelais, the word *graves* has come to be synonymous with quality. Together with the slope of the land, they create the best possible conditions for drainage ; they improve the aeration of the soil, preventing it from becoming compact. The abundance of pebbles forms a loose armour on the earth's

surface, restraining the evaporation of precious moisture from the soil (as necessary to a vine's well-being as the stagnant traps of water are noxious) during hot, dry weather. At the same time, it keeps the soil fresh, shielding it from the penetration of the sun's heat, reflecting it obliquely from the pebble surfaces back to the bunches of grapes (necessarily protected by the leaves from the sun's direct rays to prevent " grilling "). This daytime reflection of heat, in combination with the heat absorbed by the pebbles during the day and emitted to warm the low-hanging grapes at night, is invaluable to precocious ripening. Because white reflects heat and black absorbs it, the blond colour of the soil at Yquem is particularly effective in protecting the earth and returning the sun's heat to the vines.

Winter view of pruned vinestocks ; the arid
gravelly clay terrain is essential to the quality of Yquem.

On most of the estate, Yquem's topsoil is a pale yellowish-grey mixture of sand and clay in which are intermingled whitish, often translucent quartz pebbles, worn and polished to smooth, flattened, more or less elliptical shapes, which account for well over half the bulk of the soil. The subsoil is mainly clay, pebbled and with a variable calcium content, beneath which is a permeable limestone foundation. On the lower part of the vineyard, to the north, in the section called "La Grave", the topsoil contains less clay, the pebbles are larger, and the clay subsoil thins out, the topsoil residing directly on the limestone bed near the boundary. These variations in soil structure from one part of the estate to

another are amongst the most important of the factors that bring to the wine of Yquem its full, intricate completeness. To paraphrase Pierre Meslier, "Several different styles of Sauternes could be made from the grapes picked on different sections of the estate; each would be a perfect wine of its kind but not one, alone, could equal Yquem for complexity and finesse". In short, Yquem is greater than the sum of its parts.

The combination of a pebbly sand and clay mixture – called *graves grasses* because of the clay content – and a clay subsoil is said to be ideal for the production of great white wines, but poor for red wine. No adequate explanation can be given and it must be assumed that the observation is based simply on the fact that Château d'Yquem issues from such a combination.

A *forty-year-old Sémillon vinestock after pruning,*
secured to the lowest wire with willow twigs.

*Two views of the vineyard before pruning
on a sunny December day.*

The vineyard at the approach of picking (left-hand page).

Many have sought the answer to the unique quality of Yquem in its soil, none more convincingly than the nineteenth century agronomist, Petit-Lafitte, and it is doubtful that anyone has analysed Yquem's soil structure more thoroughly: "It is certain that a fundamental difference exists between the wines of Yquem and those of the other great growths of the Ciron valley ... It is very likely that the reason for this great difference must be searched out in the subsoil of Yquem, in the proximity of this subsoil, in the clay that is its principal constituent. By a geological exception quite rare in the Graves region, the vineyard of Yquem reposes on a subsoil of clay, variable in colour but principally brownish-yellow, mingled above all with smooth rounded stones and sometimes with more or less abundant fragments of chalk. The gravel that covers this subsoil rarely surpasses a depth of 30 cm (1 ft) at any place on the domain. Before depositing their charge, the diluvial currents that swept these stones along the left bank of the Garonne, from Langon to Lesparre, first depleted the surface strata of the tertiary formation, working on the clay and even the marl. This is why, everywhere else, when one uncovers the subsoil, one discovers either marl, solid enough to have resisted these forces, or more commonly limestone. At Yquem, and for special reasons that it would be difficult to explain, the strata of clay have been spared and it is upon this foundation, forming today the gracious mound that is the château's base, that has been spread a thin layer of pebbles."

Petit-Lafitte has also broken down the physical structure of the topsoil at Yquem, which is described as yellowish in colour, into four categories: pebbles (at least 5 mm [1/4 in]: 55 %); gravel (at least 3 mm [1/8 in]: 11 %); sand (18 %) and powder (16 %). All categories are described as "silicious, rounded, polished" and the powder as "quite rough" to the touch and, when examined through a magnifying glass, composed of "rounded, translucent grains, many very small".

Petit-Lafitte's analysis of the mineral content of Yquem's soil is: chalk, 1.4 %; silica (pebbles, gravel and sand), 69 %; clay, 23.8 %; iron, 5.8 %. He notes that the humus content is very low.

The same author suggests tentatively that the presence of certain unusual weeds in a vineyard, although not in itself beneficial to the vines, may be an indication of the quality of the wine. At Yquem, in particular, the uncommon abundance of wild calendula (*souci des champs*) is noted as well as a "botanical monstrosity", lamb's lettuce (*mâche*), whose flowers have an unnatural formation.

A climate tempered by the ocean's proximity, a mound of arid, reflecting pebbles reposing upon a cushion of clay at the juncture of two rivers, protected from ocean winds by a bank of pine forest – these are the specific, eccentric gifts of nature, assembled by chance or by predestined miracle, that permit Yquem to be what it is. Superimposed upon this framework, shifting weather conditions – the amount and the seasonal distribution of the sun, the rains, the winds and the temperatures of each growing season – shape the individual personality of each vintage.

To this complex of natural conditions, rendered more perfect or less perfect by erratic seasonal caprices, there is little that man can donate beyond the attentions that smooth the way for the mechanism to operate unhindered. The meagre amount of compost added is not aimed at altering the soil structure but at maintaining a natural equilibrium of respectable poverty without its becoming sterile ; in unusual years, when the autumn mists have failed to arrive on time, attempts have been made to simulate the early morning humidity by laying, between the rows of vines, water pipes that emit a fine spray – the results are described by Alexandre de Lur Saluces as " inconclusive ".

The only real amelioration to the natural structure is the subterranean installation of a prodigious network – some 100 kilometres (62 miles) – of terracotta drainage pipes. This forms an invaluable adjunct to the natural draining properties of the stony slope because of the varying permeability of the clay subsoil which, without reinforced drainage, would allow pockets of water to be retained in certain parts of the vineyard. Plans for the present installation were made by Romain-Bertrand de Lur Saluces, but the work was not carried out until after his death, the largest part during the years 1883-6. Today, these pipes – easily located thanks to a detailed map of the entire network – are repaired or replaced each year when and where vines are torn up, that is to say, on an average of once every forty-five years.

Before the installation of this network of pipes, the refinement of the natural drainage was achieved by burying bundles of pine branches in trenches to create drainage tunnels throughout the vineyard.

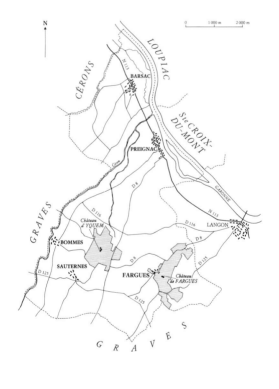

Map of Sauternes indicating
the estates of Château d'Yquem and Château de Fargues.

59

YQUEM AND THE GREAT VINEYARD CRISES

The greatest wines of the modern world are made from grapes whose vines have evolved, over the last couple of millenia, through a combination of natural and human selection, in such intimate harmony with a given climate, microclimate and soil structure, the character of each modified, moulded and refined by the exigencies of these regional particularities, that the vine and its habitat have become inseparable. So it is with Riesling on the Banks of the Rhine, Pinot-Noir and Chardonnay on the slopes of the Côte d'Or, Merlot and the Cabernets throughout the Bordelais, and Sémillon and Sauvignon in Graves and Sauternes (a third variety, Muscadelle, is planted in small quantities in some Sauternes vineyards but there is no record of its having ever existed at Yquem).

Latin writers and fossilized vine stumps are witnesses to the fact that the cultivation of wine grapes was well established in the Bordelais at the beginning of the Christian era. Ancient documents, however, are frustratingly scarce. By the mid-seventeenth century, the concept of individual great growths amongst the Bordeaux wines, though perhaps already in an embryonic state, had not yet come of age ; wines were commercialized according to their general region of origin. In a document dated 1647 [13] the prices quoted for Sauternes were the highest for all of the Bordeaux white wines and surpassed the reds of Graves and the Médoc. A manuscript from the Bordeaux municipal library [14], dated fifty years later, confirms that " It is the white wines that sell dearly – it is very expensive to cultivate them ... ".

In written records, Château d'Yquem's reputation as " le premier vin blanc de Bordeaux " seems to have sprung full-blown into being during the eighteenth century (that of " le premier vin blanc du monde " emerged a century later), mute testimony that the property had for long been producing fine wine, for such reputations are not born overnight.

Spraying for mildiou,
early summer (left-hand page).

Viticultural literature is, for the most part, a history of prolonged crises punctuated by brief moments of euphoria, both being kindled most often by political and economic circumstances. But the last half of the nineteenth century witnessed a series of physical disasters, the most dramatic of which were the successive appearances of three hitherto unknown enemies of the vine : oïdium (powdery mildew), phylloxera and mildiou (downy mildew). Each contributed to a fundamental change in the structure of the vineyards and even in the concept of viticulture.

Oïdium

Oïdium is a fungus disease which attacks the surfaces of the tender green parts of the plant – young branches, leaves and fruit – dusting them first with white, powdery spores, then blackening the young wood and reducing the unripened grapes to ugly, dried and blackened parchment. It was first observed in England, in 1845, on greenhouse grapes. (At least, that is the generally accepted story and it was the English who named it ; many believe that it arrived in England from America, but one Bordeaux writer claims that it was first observed in the Gironde as early as 1834.) Officially, its presence in the Bordelais was first noted in 1851 at Podensac, a few kilometres distant from Sauternes and, a year later, it was recognized as a serious menace. It was successfully treated by blowing sulphur powder onto the vines – but this treatment was only found after a couple of helpless years of frustration and it was a decade before it was generally applied in a rational way. For most growers failed to realize that its effect was largely preventative and that its powers to arrest the malady were slight and thus, at first, treatments were not begun until the disease was already in evidence [15]. The parasite thrives on humidity : in a good year with a warm spring and a sunny dry summer, two or three early preventative treatments will ward it off for the year, but cold, damp and rainy years may require repeated treatments and still fail to control it.

Until the mid-nineteenth century, Sauvignon may have been the dominant grape variety at Yquem – it is certain that it was proportionally more important than it is at present [16]. During the 1850s, partly because Sémillon had proven much more resistant to oïdium than Sauvignon, and partly because of its greater susceptibility to noble rot, Sémillon began to be given more space in the vineyard. It began also to soar in peoples' esteem. Quoting Mas and Pulliat (*Le Vignoble*, 1874), who had characterized Sémillon as " le grand cépage blanc français ", the *Traité général d'ampélographie* (Viala and Vermorel, 1910) continues, " Never has a qualification been more justified, for it alone can produce the perfect example of the greatest white wines in the world and, agriculturally, it is the most satisfactory of varieties. In red vineyards no variety possesses the same multiplicity of qualities, whether from the point of view of abundance or for the perfection of the product. "

Phylloxera

In 1864 the vine root louse, phylloxera, arrived in the south of France on cuttings of American wild grape vines. The catastrophic implications of this little accident were only spelt out as vineyards began to disappear, first in France, then the world over, for it spread rapidly. Although certain species of American wild vines had apparently always lived with it in immunity, it is lethal to the European wine vine whose several thousand varieties all belong to a single species, *vitis vinifera*. The louse attaches itself to the roots, leeches the vine's sustenance and leaves a poisoned and unhealable wound. The leaves wither and fall and the vine dies.

As early as 1871, scientists recommended grafting European vines onto American wild vine rootstocks as a possible solution. In the early 1870s, the Bordeaux botanist, Millardet, studied the properties of the various wild American grape species and varieties, their adaptability to grafting and to different soils and, at the same time, created a number of new rootstocks through hybridizations of American vines.

During these same years, other researchers perfected a treatment which, although it could not eradicate phylloxera, appeared to hold it at bay. It was an expensive, dangerous and complicated process which involved the injection of carbon disulphide, a powerful insecticide, into the earth. In the beginning, the P.L.M. (Chemins de Fer de Paris à Lyon et à la Méditerranée) furnished and shipped it to all of France and sent out specialists from Marseille to train *vignerons* in its application. It was delivered in the form of a liquid contained in metal drums ; a booklet of instructions published by P.L.M. contained warnings to the effect that it was inflammable, its vapours were dangerous to breathe and that, in combination with air, it formed an explosive substance. Workers were enjoined not to smoke : " They must be made to understand absolutely that the vapours are far-reaching and that the slightest spark can cause a formidable explosion. " The earth was treated during the winter and in the spring just before the flowering of the vine, twice each time, at intervals of several days, with a large injector containing the heavy liquid which, upon entering the earth, was transformed into a gas. It was recommended that the earth neither be worked ahead of the treatment, nor for at least fifteen days following it, and that the holes made by the injector be well and immediately plugged up. (Potassium thiocarbonate, poured in solution into the soil, was also used but its application was even more difficult as it involved the transport of vast quantities of water to all parts of the vineyard.)

Although resistance to grafting the indigenous *vinifera* vines onto wild American roots was less violent and irrational than in Burgundy, where it was momentarily outlawed, the prestigious growths remained firmly opposed. Anything seemed preferable to the uprooting of the old vines, whose age alone was a far from negligible factor in the quality of the wines and, quite naturally, they feared an irremediable loss of quality from an infusion of coarse blood into the noble *vinifera* veins. The study and creation of rootstocks was, moreover, only at its beginnings and, as long as the old vines could be partially maintained, it was politic to await the further development and perfection of rootstocks and to observe their performance in neighbouring vineyards. A vine, once planted, was expected to pass the half-century mark and a mistake due to too hasty a decision could lead to a loss of many years of production.

Yquem was lucky. The sandy soils of Sauternes (cushioned by the sandy soils of the surrounding Graves region) proved to be a deterrent to the louse's progress. It had arrived in the Gironde in 1869 and in Graves, not far from Sauternes, in 1875, but did not

Budding grape bunch before flowering.

A Sémillon vinestock in May (right-hand page).

penetrate Sauternes itself until 1879, sixteen years after its first appearance in France; even then, the sandy soil, uncongenial to phylloxera, attenuated the violence of the attack. Sixteen years of assiduous observation and analysis of the experiments, failures and relative successes in fighting the louse in other vineyards was an enormous advantage. The long-term results of grafting remained an imponderable, and carbon disulphide had already proved to be effective elsewhere – the possibility of a choice did not exist. By the turn of the century, the inevitability of replacing the old vines by grafting Sémillon and Sauvignon cuttings onto American rootstock was recognized but, in order to maintain a production of quality, the treatments of the old vines on native roots were continued with gradual annual replacements of grafted vines.

The total reconstitution of the vineyard dates only from the years following the First World War and, at no time, was there a noticeable slump in production due to phylloxera. The observation that " 1878 was the last great pre-phylloxera vintage ", a cliché all too familiar to wine lovers, is patently untrue – and the continuing suspicion today that pre-phylloxera wines were better than those that followed is unfounded. Because of the tardy and very gradual transition to grafted vines, the famous Yquem vintages of 1899 and 1900 issued only from the old vines on their original roots – the grafted vines already in place were not old enough to be used in the *grand vin*. A restrained but increasing seepage of grapes from grafted vines entered into the pre-First World War Yquems; 1921, the most celebrated vintage of this century, was also amongst the first to be made in large part from grafted vines.

MILDIOU

It is true – but most particularly for red wines – that 1878 marks the end of a twenty-year run of spectacular vintages known as *l'âge d'or* or *la belle époque*; it also marks the appearance in France of mildiou, another fungus disease, more insidious than oïdium in that it penetrates the tissues of the young wood, hibernates in the dormant buds and eventually destroys the vine. It came with American vine cuttings intended for use in the development of rootstocks to control phylloxera; it appeared in the Bordelais in 1881.

Millardet, in collaboration with the Bordeaux chemist and œnologist, Gayon, perfected the treatment, still used in many vineyards today, of using a spray solution of copper sulphate and quick lime, known as *bouillie bordelaise* or Bordeaux mixture. As with sulphur when it was first used to combat oïdium thirty years earlier, results in the beginning were disappointing because growers waited for the malady to manifest itself before treating the vines; the Bordeaux mixture must be used preventatively from early spring onwards with a frequency dictated by the weather. (Sulphur has never been replaced as a treatment for oïdium, but a number of products have recently been developed for the control of mildiou. Pierre Meslier, who believes that a century of copper sulphate treatments has left an unnatural residue of copper in vineyard soils, prefers to alternate applications of one or another of the modern fungicides " so that the vines never become accustomed to a single product ".)

Sauternes was not immune but, once again, it was lucky for the Sémillon and Sauvignon vines both proved to be relatively resistant to mildiou. During the last two decades of the nineteenth century which, because of the effects of mildiou, were generally disastrous for the red growths, Yquem none the less produced a half-dozen vintages that have entered into twentieth-century wine literature's list of greats and it managed regularly to fetch prices well above those of the Médoc first growths. *La seigneurie et le vignoble de Château Latour* cites the following prices per *tonneau* (900 litres) for the year 1897 – the vintage was admittedly a low point for the reds : Yquem, 4,000 francs ; Mouton, 1,100 francs ; Latour, 700 francs ; Margaux, 450 francs ; Lafite, 450 francs.

ROOTSTOCKS

One of the most dramatic results of the phylloxera scourge was the emergence of a completely new branch of viticulture, that of producing rootstock and of creating new rootstocks through hybridization. Although the character of the *vinifera* grapes is not tainted by grafting, as many feared that it might be, much of the vine's comportment is affected by the traits of the wild vine or hybrid whose root nourishes it. The wild grapes have evolved in a very different milieu from that of the stony, arid, alkaline soils native to the *vinifera* roots and fine wines. In a soil to its liking, the relative vigour of the species that furnishes the rootstock will be transferred to the grafted vine. The root affects the time of flowering, the fecundation, the abundance of fruit and the time of ripening. An excessively vigorous plant will waste its strength on luxurious vegetation at the expense of the fruit. There is a risk that the fruiting will be erratic, and the grapes will be late to ripen with higher acid and lower sugar levels. For this reason it is especially important not to join a naturally vigorous *vinifera* variety, such as Sauvignon, to a vigorous rootstock. The relationship between the rootstock and *vinifera* variety is expected ideally to encourage a moderate foliation and a relatively short vegetative cycle. A certain affinity between the scion and the rootstock is essential to the join of the graft but, also in the interest of restraining vigour, that affinity should not be too great.

From the many species of American wild grape vine, three, each of which count a number of varieties, were chosen as being particularly adaptable, *vitis riparia, vitis rupestris* and *vitis berlandieri. Riparia* roots well, grafts easily and encourages fecundation and early ripening ; its limited affinity is evident in the faster-growing rate of the *vinifera* plant which eventually bulges out thickly at the graft from a much narrower root stem. Its greatest drawback is an inability to support calcium, whose presence in the soil causes the yellowing malady known as chlorosis in *riparia*-grafted vines. The other two species are naturally more vigorous and have a greater affinity to *vinifera* vines, but they also have a greater tolerance for calcium. Crossed with *riparia*, the vigour is attenuated.

The rootstocks used at Yquem are : *riparia* ; 3 309 (a *riparia* x *rupestris* hybrid) ; and 420-A (*a berlandieri* x *riparia* hybrid). The 3 309 also grafts easily and is a good companion to the untemperamental Sémillon, but is too vigorous for Sauvignon, often causing *coulure*, an ineffectual pollination which leads to the unfertilized embryo grapes falling to the ground. The 420-A has the highest tolerance for calcium of the three, and it likes gravel and clay, both abundant elements in Yquem's soil ; a higher proportion of grafts fail to take and must be replaced the following year.

Elsewhere in the Bordelais new plantations are made with year-old grafted nursery plants. The tradition in Sauternes is to plant out the chosen rootstocks one year and to graft on the *vinifera* cuttings the following year. At Yquem, to effect a continuing genetic improvement within the vineyard, the best vines – perfectly healthy, but neither too vigorous nor too productive – are chosen at the time of each season's vintage and marked to be used for eventual cutting stock. Later, in the course of winter pruning, cuttings will be taken for grafting from those vines that have been marked for superior performance during several consecutive years.

THE VINEYARD TODAY

The old vines on their own roots were longer-lived, often passing the century mark, than those grafted onto American roots. Their root systems were more complex and penetrated more deeply into the earth's substructures. At the beginning of the grafting experience this could not be foreseen but, thanks to the very gradual transition to grafted vines at Yquem, a rational restructuring of the vineyard, which evolved into an annual, cyclical system of uprooting old vines and making new plantations, was under way from the start. About 90 of the 102 hectares (220 out of 252 acres) of vineyard are always in production. The remainder consists of land lying fallow, reposing before being replanted anew, and of young vines not yet in production.

In the past, the soil had to be left for several years, planted repeatedly to nitrogenous crops that were ploughed under, to recover from the noxious effects of fragments of rotting roots that remained in it and to regain its equilibrium. Now it is treated, immediately after the vines are torn up, by injections of disinfectant products, then manured and left fallow for two years to retrieve a biological balance before being newly planted. Today, new vines are back in production six years after the old ones have been torn up.

In order to maintain an average age of twenty-five years amongst the vines in production, 2 or 3 hectares (5 to 7 acres) of vines are uprooted each year and a roughly equivalent area is planted to rooted cuttings of American vines to be grafted the following year. The vines are uprooted after about forty-five years, but old vines in good health, continuing to produce, will not be sacrificed if there are younger vines elsewhere on the property whose performance is poor; the production diminishes in old vines but theirs is the finest fruit. Here and there in the vineyard one encounters patches of vines on the decline; it is impossible to know why, for they are rarely the oldest – perhaps the rootstock is not happy with the soil at that particular spot, or the drainage may have become clogged. These vines, as well as parcels of old vines where the density of healthy vines has been reduced by mortality, will be the next to go. Complantation – the replacement of individual dead vines in plots of otherwise healthy, young, or mature, but not old vines – is also practised.

There were other modifications to the vineyard structure. In the old pattern of plantation, the vines were planted in alternating double and single rows and, with the establishment of the Sémillon predominance, every fifth plant within each row was Sauvignon, preceded and followed by four of Sémillon (but, if individual vines were replaced, they were always replaced by Sémillon); each vine was trained on a single high stake, the long, supple branches gathered together and tied near the top of the stake to form a *bouffant*.

*Young vine grafted with paraffin to American rootstock,
seen against its stake.*

*Planting root stocks ; they will not be grafted
until the following year.*

Within the rows, the vines were planted 1 metre (3 1/4 ft) apart, the double rows were separated by 85 cm (33 in) and the distance between double and single rows was 2 metres (6 1/2 ft). The soil was rarely treated with compost – every ten years – spread down the centre of the two-metre stretches and entrenched deeply to nourish the far-reaching *vinifera* roots.

The feeling that, for the wine to achieve perfection in its genre, all – or nearly all – of the grapes in the vineyard should be affected by noble rot led to a greater awareness of the fungus's requirements. A generalized insemination of the botrytis spores demands a well-aerated vineyard. In the traditional plantations, both the double rows and the system of tying the vines up on stakes blocked the free circulation of air. A maximum aeration is now assured, first, by the present pattern of planting, shifted in detail but without altering the approximate number of 7,000 vines per hectare (about 2,800 per acre): 90 cm (3 ft) between vines within the rows, 1.5 metres (5 ft) between rows with every fourth space measuring 2 metres (6 1/2 ft). Secondly, by training the vine's annual growth, fanned out on three levels of horizontal, tautly drawn wires attached to stakes that are planted within the rows at 6.5-metre (20-ft) intervals: the top wire, 120 cm (4 ft) from the ground, and the bottom wire, 40 cm (16 in) from the ground, are stationary; the intermediate level consists of two parallel wires that may be adjusted upwards as the growing branches, trained between them, extend.

Because of the less-extensive development of grafted rootstock, the vines are now treated with compost – mixed manure and humus discharged to either side, in the 1.5-metre stretches, from a wagon drawn down the 2-metre alleys – every fifth year, more shallowly and less abundantly than in the past, on a rotational system, about one-fifth of the vines in production being treated each year.

It may seem odd, in the light of the emphasis placed on a poor soil, that it should be treated with compost; in fact, at one time it was believed that vineyard soils should never receive any enrichment except to return to them the *marc* left from pressing the grapes. By the eighteenth century, discreet treatment with compost was traditional: Thomas Jefferson notes, "They dung a little in Médoc and Grave, because of the poverty of the soil; but very little as more would affect the wine." Then, as now, it was believed that the vine must be made to suffer to give of its best; it is, none the less, a living thing and requires a modicum of nourishment.

The final structural transition – the division of the Sémillon and the Sauvigon vines into separate plantations – did not take place until after the Second World War. In a mixed plantation, it was impossible to profit fully from the Sauvignon grape's particular qualities. Because Sauvignon is more susceptible to oïdium and because it buds somewhat later than Sémillon, the two varieties are best treated differently and at different times; they adapt best to different rootstocks and they require different pruning. Whereas Sémillon should be transformed by noble rot when picked, the Sauvignon is now preferred very ripe but, for the most part, unrotted so that its very personal style of fruit can lend a certain freshness to the wine.

Finally, a better control can be maintained over the balance of the finished wine if the two varieties are picked and vinified separately.

The débourrement *(budding),*
the feuillaison *(leafing), a young shoot,*
the sortie *(appearance of the flower buds).*

Works
and Days

To possess a complete understanding of Yquem's exceptional character, one must enter into the life of the vine, familiarize oneself with its plant cycle and with the cyclical tasks that follow its dictates – of which the special and different methods of pruning the two grape varieties are of primary importance – and which terminate each year with the harvest.

THE VINE'S CYCLE

The tears. The pattern of the annual work cycle is determined by the plant cycle of the vine whose renaissance is heralded each spring around mid-March by *les pleurs* (the tears), a signal that the sap has begun to well up as the unhealed winter pruning cuts brim over, the crystalline droplets falling upon the ground in such abundance that the innocent observer, encountering this phenomenon for the first time, may be troubled by the conviction that the vine is bleeding to death.

The vine's revival is then punctuated in rapid succession by the following stages of unfolding growth :

The budding. Towards the end of March, comes *le débourrement* (the budding), in which the " eyes " on the pruned branches begin to swell, splitting and shedding their protective husks (and exposing themselves to the dangers of spring frosts). These eyes, or buds, are the tiny protrusions which were born at the base of each sprouting leaf on the previous season's new growth, a year earlier, and have lain dormant until this moment ; within each eye resides the mysterious power to create a new branch – or a new vine – in all of its patterned, formal complexity.

The leafing. In early April, comes *la feuillaison* (the leafing), when the swelling eyes, or embryo branches, have stretched to tender shoots and the first miniscule leaves begin to appear, springing at intervals from the tip of the extending shoot, alternately to one side, then to the other. At the same time, barely visible new eyes appear, nestled at the V-shaped joint of the shoot and the concave, inside base of each leaf's stem ; these eyes will lie dormant throughout the growing season, only to burst forth the following year after the winter's rest and a new flood of tears.

The appearance of the flower buds. A couple of weeks later, coinciding usually with the appearance of the fourth leaf, comes *la sortie* (the emergence of the flower buds). At the same point where each leaf has sprung, but to the opposite side of the branch, a tendril forms and, on each young branch, a couple of these tendrils – rarely more – will be fertile, developing flower buds in miniature replica of bunches of grapes. (As the branches continue to push out leaf after leaf, corresponding tendrils form to the opposite side of the branch from each leaf, but these tendrils are all sterile, their role being to grasp any narrow object in their path, winding around it to secure support for the mounting vine.)

The fertilization. From *la sortie* to *la fleuraison* (the flowering) well over a month passes during which time the vine's exuberant growth continues undiminished. Flowering commonly occurs during the second week of June, but may take place as early as late May or it may drag into July ; it may last a few days or, in uncertain weather, several weeks – the grower hopes for a rapid and relatively early flowering. It is a critical moment : the potential harvest having already been deliberately and radically diminished through short pruning and sparse use of compost, the desired production now depends on the successful pollination of the flowers, aided by warm, dry weather and occasional gentle breezes. A partial or complete pollination failure results in *coulure,* in which the embryo fruit falls, unfertilized, to the ground. Rain at the time of flowering often causes *coulure ;* a late frost may also be responsible ; a late flowering, preceded by cold weather and coinciding suddenly with warm or hot weather can inspire a sudden rush of sap that may lead to massive *coulure.* Even under apparently ideal flowering conditions, its excessive vigour renders Sauvignon (which flowers slightly later than Sémillon) particularly susceptible to *coulure.* The results of *coulure* can, at worst, leave a vine completely barren for the season ; at best, the quality of the wine may not be compromised (although a meagre bunch of grapes eventually discourages the spread of noble rot from one grape to another) but the quantity will be severely curtailed.

Another condition, *millerandage,* the result of imperfect fertilization, often provoked by a prolonged flowering period, produces grape bunches containing a portion of stunted grapes that never grow to a normal size and ripen later than the other grapes on the bunch.

The setting of the fruit. La nouaison (the setting or formation of the fruit) stretches from the time of pollination until a moment falling most often between 10 and 15 August. The hard, green grapes swell in size from pin-heads to marbles without a noticeable change in their chemical make-up ; like the leaves, their chlorophyll content permits them to absorb much of their nourishment from the air ; the vine continues to grow, branches lengthening, leaves growing larger and new leaves springing forth.

Ripening and lignification. Then, quite abruptly, the vine's entire metabolic pattern shifts : from one day to another, the grapes begin to ripen ; this is *la veraison* (the ripening). Simultaneously, *l'aoûtement* (the lignification), so-called because its beginnings are in August *(août),* sets in, the supple branches turning progressively stiff and woody and darkening in colour from the base outwards. Growth slows to a near stop as all of the vine's energy is transferred to the maturation of the grapes and the wood. The chlorophyll disappears from the grapes and they draw their sugar from the leaves as, daily, the acidity diminishes and the sugar content rises. The grapes are said to be ripe a hundred days after flowering – it is a handy but only very approximate figure ; the Sauvignon catches up with the Sémillon during the growing season and both ripen at the same time.

When the leaves have done their work, they begin to turn colour and gradually to fall from the vine ; by the early days of November the last leaves have fallen, the lignification of the branches has been completed, the sap is descending and the vine will lie dormant until the tears flow again.

THE WORK CYCLE

The end of the plant cycle normally marks the beginning of the annual work cycle. At Yquem, the leaves may have fallen before the last grapes, long since ripened and barely nourished by the vine but still insufficiently withered by the external influence of noble rot, are picked ; the new work cycle will begin when the work force is freed from picking and cellar work.

As soon as the last grapes are picked, the 2 or 3 hectares (5 to 7 acres) of old vines to be destroyed are uprooted by tractors, the topsoil is ploughed deeply to aerate it and all possible root fragments are removed. The drainage system is cleaned and repaired, any broken pipes being replaced. The soil is sterilized, treated with compost and left fallow.

Fallow vineyard ready for replanting is manured, ploughed, raked and staked out in readiness for the new spring plantations. Here, the manuring will be more generous than for vines in production ; it is true that a mature vine must be made to suffer to give its best but it must, above all, not be made to suffer in tender youth – if not pampered in its formative, pre-production years, it will never grow up to suffer in glory.

About 18 hectares (45 acres) of vines in production, their time having come round for the five-yearly ration, will be discreetly treated with organic compost and humus. The 90 hectares (225 acres) of vineyard in production will be ploughed between the rows, soil being thrown up around the base of the vines to protect the roots and grafts from winter cold – the feet of the vines are said to be *chaussées,* or shod. This late autumn or early winter ploughing is the first of the labours of the vineyard soil known as *les façons.*

WINTER PRUNING

The vine is a vagabond thing. Unless its growth is severely restrained and disciplined, it will wander aimlessly, climbing here, creeping there, extending its reach and multiplying its tentacles year after year, draining itself of its strength and, if permitted to do so, producing hundreds of bunches of useless sour grapes that never ripen.

The winter pruning, which takes place in January and February, and the way in which

it is done is perhaps the single most critical and exacting task consecrated to the vine: the quality of the harvest and the health of the plant depend on it. There are many styles of pruning, the particular form that each takes being imposed by the climate, the characteristics of the grape variety, the relative vigour of the rootstock, the soil structure, the age of the vine, and by local traditions. All aim at maintaining a physical and metabolic equilibrium in the plant and at limiting production. Severe prunings – within commonsense limits – will produce the richest grapes, the most precocious ripening and the best wines.

Each year's new growth must spring from the dormant eyes formed on the newly lignified branches of the preceding season. As a matter of principle, it is accepted that only the shoots that develop from these eyes will be fertile (this is usually but not always true) and, in any case, it is only by respecting this principle that the form and health of the vine can be correctly maintained. The rejects or suckers, parasitic shoots growing from invisible eyes in the old wood, are systematically removed during the growing season unless one is needed to re-form the vine at winter-pruning time the following year. Whatever the variations from one style of pruning to another, the underlying tenet

The floraison *(flowering), beginning of the* nouaison
(setting of the fruit) on a bunch that has suffered coulure,
end of the nouaison, *the* véraison *(ripening).*

Gathering the branches at the time of winter pruning (right-hand page).

76

imposes the complete elimination of a portion of the previous year's branches, while those remaining are severed at points designed to retain only those eyes necessary to produce the same number of branches that have just been removed or cut back.

The cutting instruments – secateur for the new growth and small pruning saw for the old wood – must be sharp ; the cuts must be clean and those on the old wood neatly trimmed to hasten healing. The cut will be angled obliquely to avoid collecting rainwater, which rots the wood, and positioned with the bias to the opposite side from the nearest

eye so that " its tears may not drop upon the budding eye and blind it "[17].

The vinestock. Over a period of several years, each newly planted young vine must be pruned in such a way as to create its basic trunk or stock formation, the *cep*, or grisly stump, from which, as it grows thicker and more gnarled year after year for close upon half a century, the pruner will snip back the preceding year's growth and direct that of the season to come. In a temperate climate where spring frosts are not the norm, and particularly where the terrain is heavily pebbled as at Yquem, these vinestocks are formed close to the ground so that, during the ripening season, the low-hanging grapes may profit

Pruning Sémillon vines. The severed branches hang loosely from the wires.

The branches are burned in the vineyard.

during cool nights from the reflected heat that the stones have absorbed from the sun during the day.

The basic, perennial form of the vinestock is the same for both Sémillon and Sauvignon ; two short, uplifted arms are trained from each bole, in alignment with the row of vines, to fashion a stubby Y-shape of old wood, from the extremities of which spring each year's new growth.

Finally, despite general styles of pruning, each vine must be treated as an individual with different needs[18]. An experienced pruner with a sure intuition and a sharp eye understands, at a glance, the needs of each vine, envisaging the future form that the secateur's scissions will impose upon its seasonal growth ; there is no time to ponder for, after the coldest part of the winter and before the sap begins to rise – and when the weather permits – some 630,000 mature vines plus several tens of thousands of young vines in formation must be pruned.

Some prunings are said to be short and others long ; the chosen style depends upon the eccentricities of the vine in question. Since the separation of the Sauvignon vines from the Sémillon, Yquem has practised both styles.

Sémillon. Sémillon, which is only a moderately vigorous vine, untemperamental and, by nature, an abundant producer, is pruned short. All of the previous season's growth is removed except for three branches whose positions, as close to the old wood as possible, are carefully chosen so that the new shoots will fan out along the row and in alignment with the wires to which they will be attached. Each of these three branches is cut back to a stump on which two visible eyes remain (an ill-formed and nearly invisible eye at the joint of the branch and the old wood often produces a frail, sterile shoot that is removed in the spring). This style is called *the taille à côts*, a *côt* being a branch cut short to either two or three eyes. It is the same as that practised on all the vines at Yquem in the last century, before the arrival of phylloxera, except that the vines were pruned to two instead of three *côts*, each with three instead of two eyes.

Sauvignon. An exceptionally vigorous vine promotes an exuberant foliation at the expense of the fruit ; the sap seems to race to the furthest extremities of its unfurling ramifications without pause along the way to adequately nourish its nearer constituents, and the young growth closest to the old wood is the least privileged. It might be thought that a short pruning could harness and control all this energy, but in fact it appears only to intensify the rush of sap to the tips of the young shoots. The first couple of eyes on a branch – those closest to the vinestock – often produce shoots that are sterile ; when they are not, the embryo bunches of grapes are especially subject to *coulure*. Such is the case with the Sauvignon vines and it can easily be understood that, when they are pruned in the same way as the Sémillon, their comportment is a source of great frustration.

The Sauvignon vines that are over thirty years old, still intermingled in the old plantations, are inevitably pruned in the same way as the Sémillon for, in the absence of leaves, the pruner can too easily mistake one variety for another. The separate plantations of Sauvignon are now pruned to one long branch reaching from one of the arms of the vinestock. This is called an *aste* ; it may be cut to as many as eight eyes but at Yquem it is limited to six. A *côt* with two eyes is left on the other arm ; one of the two

*Sharpening the pruning shears. The subtle art of
guiding horses with a secret language.*

branches, both usually infertile, that spring from these eyes will be chosen at pruning time a year hence for the following year's *aste*. In this way, the fruit-bearing branches are borne in alternating years, first by one arm, then by the other. Because a vertical branch is always more vigorous than one trained horizontally, the *aste* will be attached horizontally to the lowest wire, curbing its vigour and encouraging the formation and the ripening of fruit. This method is known as *Guyot simple*. If applied to Sémillon vines, the first eyes of whose branches dependably produce fertile shoots, it would lead to overproduction, but it is an admirable solution for the cantankerous Sauvignon. The *taille à côts*, applied to the Sémillon vines, permits the development of six branches, all of which, under normal circumstances, are expected to produce fruit; the *Guyot simple* gives eight branches to the Sauvignon but only four or five are expected to be fertile.

In the course of the winter pruning, the most perfectly lignified branches, taken from the vines that have been chosen during several consecutive harvests for quality performance and marked for reproduction, are set aside. Because the extremities of a branch never lignify perfectly, only the lower portions of the branches are saved; they will be stored beneath dry sand until the time comes, a month or two later, for grafting.

While the men prune, the women follow behind, gathering together the severed branches, still loosely hanging from the wires; a few are bundled to provide firewood throughout the year for grilling meats – most are thrown onto fires in the alleys separating the rows of vines.

When pruning is finished, the men go through the vineyard to replace stakes that are the worse for wear and to tighten the wires.

Popaul and
Pompon with their groom.
Traditional ploughing (right-hand page).

In *spring the parallel double wires*
are shifted progressively upwards to train the young shoots.

The effeuillage, *or defoliation (right-hand page).*

In March the vineyard is again ploughed between the rows; the vines are *déchaussées*, unshod, and the soil between the vines within each row loosened up by hoeing, care being taken not to damage the roots or the vinestock. Throughout the growing season, periodic shallow tillings, their frequency determined by the weather, will be carried out to destroy the weeds that suck nourishment and moisture from the earth and to rupture the capillary system, formed by the earth's crust, that encourages the evaporation of the soil's store of moisture.

During March and April the new plantations of rooted cuttings of American rootstock, furnished by specialized nurseries, are set out; and those planted the preceding year are grafted with the *vinifera* cuttings that have been held in sand since pruning, first cut into lengths bearing two eyes each and briefly soaked in water. Rootstock plantations from the preceding year that have not taken are replaced and plants whose year-old grafts have not taken are grafted anew.

Treatments. Preventative treatments against oïdium, mildiou and other diseases and pests begin at the time of leafing with a *soufrage*, or sulphuring, and, a week or so later, with the first spraying of fungicide. Because the air circulation created by blowing sulphur on the vines is an aid to pollination, the moment of flowering is usually chosen for the second sulphur treatment (the exception to the rule that all activity in the vines must cease during flowering), another spraying being reserved for later. Two or three sulphurings are often enough for the season and, in a year of fine weather, the same may be true of spraying; a rainy spring and summer, on the other hand, may impose new treatments each time the vines are washed clean.

The suppression of young suckers (l'épamprage). During the couple of months preceding the flowering a number of unwanted shoots or *gourmands* (suckers) push out from beneath the bark of the vinestock. They are parasitic in the sense that they draw nourishment from the vine that should be reserved for the fertile shoots issuing from the last season's wood. Except for the occasional sucker necessary for the re-formation of a vinestock at the following winter's pruning, they are all eliminated; when still very tender in April or May, a flick of the fingers is all that is necessary to snap them free.

Attaching the vines (le palissage) and *summer pruning* (le rognage). The arms of the vinestock and the *astes* of the Sauvignon vines are tied to the bottom wire with willow twigs. The women pass several times through the vineyard during the month of June and the first part of July, training the fragile young shoots between the double wires and shifting these upwards as growth continues, tying the branches loosely to the top wires with lengths of rush; some may also be tied to the central wires to spread them out fanwise.

By the last part of July the growth will have become so profuse that it must be cut back, both to keep the passages between the rows unencumbered and to redirect the sap from the continuously forming new leaves back to the grapes. This *rognage*, or pruning, should remove no more of the mature leaves than necessary, for their presence is essential both to the ripening of the grapes and to the proper lignification of the branches; a circumspect trimming will hasten ripening and improve lignification.

Pushing back the sap in this way often forces the normally dormant, furthest eyes on a branch to sprout prematurely; the shoots are snapped off at their bases as they appear.

At about the same time, if, despite all precautions to curb production, the vines bear an extraordinary abundance of grapes, the least-promising bunches are removed and discarded so as not to compromise the perfect ripening of the others; ten full bunches are the maximum that a normally healthy vine can nourish to perfection.

The defoliation (l'effeuillage). The progressive removal of leaves from the vines to a height sufficient to expose all the grape bunches to air currents and, finally, to the direct rays of the autumn sun, begins shortly before the grapes are completely ripe and continues, in most years, well into the harvest, usually being completed by the first days of October. Its most important function is to encourage the spread of noble rot by increasing aeration but, by eliminating the moisture harboured from humid autumn nights by leaf clusters, it also discourages grey rot.

During the first couple of weeks of the operation, a delicate balance must be struck for, until the grapes are completely ripened, the healthy, green leaves that continue to feed them sugar must remain undisturbed and, at the same time, the grapes should continue to be protected from the direct rays of the late summer sun. The leaves closest to the vinestock, the first-born, are the first to begin turning yellow; these, first to the north and, a few days later, to the south, are the first to go. The progressive removal of leaves continues slowly upwards until the grapes' ripening process has stabilized, no more sugar being drawn from the leaves, then it is speeded up until the vines are completely free of leaves up to the level of the highest bunch of grapes. The remaining leaves at the extremities of the branches, the last to turn, will continue to furnish sugar, in the form of starch, to the branches to perfect their lignification.

An enjambeur, *or " straddling " tractor.*

Vintage
and Vinification

It is not possible to overemphasize the importance of restrained production. Radical pruning, scanty use of compost and a predominance of old vines, in combination with the most privileged of positions and soil structures, mean that, although by comparison with the vigorous, green and luxuriant vines that lie outside its boundaries, Yquem's vines may not possess the same superficial exuberance, the few bunches of grapes that they bear ripen earlier with a higher sugar content, more intense flavour and a greater complexity of aromatic essences than those from most of the surrounding vines[19]. Weather permitting, the *vendanges*, or vintages, at Yquem regularly begin a few days earlier than elsewhere, not because they are in a hurry but because the grapes have ripened earlier and the noble rot is in a more advanced stage. (At Château de Fargues, where the vines receive the same care as those at Yquem, the vintage usually begins a week later because of the difference in soil structure.) In a precarious season, a few days' advance can be a huge bonus, meaning in extreme instances that a few barrels of perfect wine may be made before the rains set in and annihilate the remaining harvest.

The rhythm of the vintages

The dates and the hours of picking, weather permitting, and the condition of the grapes to be picked – the degree to which they are shrivelled by noble rot – are determined by the weight of the must, the level of sugar concentration.

Before the beginning of the vintage and repeatedly throughout its duration, both in the waiting periods between *tries* and several times during the pressing of each batch of grapes, samples of the must are measured with a glucometer.

*After lunch, the pickers return to the vineyard
(left-hand page).*

The appearance of the grapes, even when withered to the *rôti* stage, cannot accurately indicate their level of sugar concentration : grapes ripen every year (or nearly so), that is to say, they arrive at a stage of physiological maturity when, before advancing into various states of surmaturation from outside influences, the combined rising sugar content and descending acidity are arrested and, at the same time, the pips turn hard, deepening from a milky green colour to dark brown. But, depending on the season that has produced it, the sugar content of a grape that has reached complete physiological maturity can vary greatly. As it is this variable quantity of sugar that is subsequently partially consumed by the parasitic botrytis, the remainder being concentrated in the grape berries as they wither under the combined influences of the botrytis, the sun and the wind, it naturally follows that, from one year to another, grapes that exhibit visually the same surface effects of noble rot do not necessarily contain the same degree of concentration of sugar.

In some years, only the individual grape berries that have arrived at the shrunken *rôti* stage may be picked to achieve the correct reading of potential alcohol ; in others this concentration may be tempered by the addition of *pourris-pleins* grapes – those that are still plump but whose skins have turned brown ; finally, following unusually hot summers and especially high potential alcohol readings, it may be necessary to pick a certain proportion of grapes unaffected by botrytis – *grains verts* – in order to lower the sugar concentration of a given *trie*.

Under no circumstances, however, must the grapes be picked when they are swollen with water from outside influences. Because the skins of grapes at the *rôti* stage have become fragile and porous, their structure broken down by the digestive action of the fungus, they and the dehydrated pulp act like sponges, greedily absorbing any humidity in the atmosphere. Rain will cause the withered grapes to swell with water and the sugar count will fall disastrously ; sunny weather or dry winds are necessary to redehydrate them before they can be picked. Their thirst is quenched also by the morning mists and, even in perfect weather, the picking must wait until an hour or so of sun has evaporated

A *picker's pannier, gloves and secateur ; the joints of the pannier, like those of the* comportes, *are sealed with sealing wax, lest a drop of juice be lost.*

Comportes *draining after having been rinsed at the day's end (left-hand page).*

the moisture which they have sponged up. The juice from grapes at the same stage of advancement, picked in the afternoon, often measures several degrees more potential alcohol than that of those picked in the morning.

VINTAGE DATES

Three times out of four the vintage begins during the last half of September. In 1893 it began on 28 August; in 1980 it began on 20 October. Great wine was made both years, but these are freak vintages. In 1893, the heat arrived the first of March and continued throughout the season; in 1980, early beginnings rapidly deteriorated into a

cold, rainy spring, late, imperfect flowering and a damp summer, followed by a fine month of September that permitted the grapes to ripen but not before mid-October – cold November weather and wind controlled the development of noble rot in the absence of morning mists and sunny days.

Since 1893 picking has begun only four times before 15 September (1921, 1922, 1934 and 1960). It has only twice begun later than 20 October – 26 October in 1974 and

Before lunch, a picker seeks out the bottle
of red wine bearing his name.

Pickers returning to the vineyard (preceding pages).

25 October in 1978 – but, in the first instance, there was no Yquem and in the second very little. In 1974 a perfect growing season unfurled, until 15 September when two months of rain and cold weather crushed all hopes (the seasonal pattern in 1982 was not unlike that of 1974 except that a small amount of great wine was extracted from the first two *tries* before the rains began on 2 October, compromising the remaining harvest). 1978 was a topsy-turvy season – early but sluggish spring, with late and prolonged flowering ; chilly and rainy summer ; abnormally late but extended and glorious autumn with ripening retarded a full month and stubbornly reticent botrytis – fine wines were made but only a small fraction possessed sufficient concentration for Yquem.

Prolonged pickings and oft-repeated *tries* lead to perilous hazards and huge expense ; their justification is to give all the grapes on each bunch every possible opportunity, often at the risk of losing all or part of a harvest, to wither from noble rot. The stakes are high but, when the gamble succeeds, so are the winnings. In the last twenty years the length of the vintages and the number of *tries* have varied from as few as twenty-two days and two *tries* in 1976, when it was a race with the botrytis to get the grapes in before sugar concentrations became too intense, to as many as seventy-one days and eleven *tries* in 1972, when the gamble failed, for there was no Yquem. The average is around forty-five days and five or six *tries*.

Beautiful wines are often made in difficult and atypical years but the ideal season – a relatively precocious and gentle spring ; early, rapid flowering, hot, dry summer with early and late showers ; morning mists and sunny days around mid-September, at the moment of the grapes' physiological maturity, with a rapid evolution of botrytis and a minimum of *tries* – is fortunately no rarity. With variations in detail, 1921, 1928, 1929 (exceptionally dry summer), 1934, 1937, 1943, 1945 (spring frost, reduced crop, very dry summer), 1947 (hottest summer of the century), 1949, 1959, 1967, 1970, 1975, 1976 and 1983, all classic vintages, fall pretty much into this category.

VINTAGE TIME

The simple mechanics of the *vendange* are a good bit more complex than at those vineyards where dry white wines or red wines are made from normally ripened grapes. There, the principle of picking, once the grapes have arrived at their maximum stage of maturity and on condition that they are healthy, is to clip whole bunches from the vines in one passage through the vineyard and to transport them as rapidly as possible to the *chais*, or vinification cellars. Under these circumstances, no special qualities are demanded of the picker beyond a natural inclination to move along without wasting time and the physical stamina to support the back-strain from day-long bending over.

At Yquem, experience and a sharp eye are essential. The picker must be able to tell, at a glance, which grapes on a bunch, if any, are damaged, thus carrying the threat of grey rot and bacterial alteration (these must be removed and cast away) ; which are in the noble state of sanctity, shrivelled but intact, ready to be picked ; and which, although perhaps affected by noble rot, should be left for a later *trie*. The few inexperienced pickers are trained by their fellow-workers and by the overseers, or *chefs de troupe*, with the expectation that they will return year after year ; the exacting demands do not make it

*The vines at Yquem
at the moment of the harvest.*

A *late* trie.

possible to hire itinerant workers, or students in search of a diverting experience before returning to the preparation of other careers.

With the exception of the men needed in the *chais*, all the members of the year-round workforce go into the vineyard to pick; in addition, about eighty workers from the immediate region are hired regularly for picking. They must be on call, ready to pick at a moment's notice, throughout the period of the vintage, for a *trie* may be postponed at the last minute because of threatening rain or it may be interrupted by rain; two or three days – or several weeks – of inactivity may separate the successive *tries*. If it is obvious that a week or so must pass without further picking, they are free to work elsewhere but, when the grapes at Yquem are ready, the *vendangeurs* must be ready – seven days a week. Often 120 *vendangeurs* are kept in readiness on the property as the clouds turn, threatening rain ... the clouds may suddenly shift and the rain will fall on Barsac or Fargues, then they are hustled into the vines to go to work. (If the rain falls on Yquem and not at Fargues, the entire workforce may be hastily trucked to Château de Fargues to pick there.) The workers may be asked to lunch early when it is too risky to go into the vines to pick or, if the sky clears, they may be asked to profit from a moment's certainty and to lunch late.

In a traditional vineyard – in Médoc, for instance – a *vendangeur* is normally expected to pick the equivalent of from one to two barrels of wine per day, whereas at Yquem, five to ten *vendangeurs* are required for one barrel and, in particularly difficult years, there have been up to eighty *vendangeurs* in the vineyard for the day's harvest of a single barrel of must.

Except for patches of old vines where the two grape varieties are still intermingled, the Sauvignon is picked on different days from the Sémillon and vinified separately; although it, too, is picked by *tries*, the grape berries are, ideally, ripe to the point of being somewhat withered but relatively little affected by noble rot. The Sauvignon's natural resistance to botrytis makes this possible and the fresh, fruity quality of the unaffected grapes lends a certain zest to the young wine.

In years when grey rot threatens and the noble rot has not yet arrived at a stage to justify picking, an initial *trie*, called *trie de nettoyage*, or cleansing *trie*, the removal and discard of damaged grapes, is necessary. Throughout the *vendanges*, as the nobly rotted grapes are selectively picked, the damaged grapes are removed and discarded to safeguard the future of the healthy grapes under the influence of noble rot. Visitors are astonished to see the pickers scattering their path with grapes as they advance.

When the development of the botrytis is sluggish, workers are not brought in from outside. When the full force of 120 is there, it is divided into three equal groups, each with its own *chef de troupe* to guide and direct the pickers. Each group is sent to a different part of the vineyard so that, as the grapes arrive at the *chai*, those born of variable soil structures will be fused in the pressing.

The pickers, for the most part women, are each equipped with a small wooden pannier and smaller-than-usual, narrow-bladed, sharply pointed pruning shears. A tractor-drawn dray, upon which are piled a tarpaulin and twelve to fifteen *comportes* – half-barrel-like hods with wooden rod handles extending to either side – is stationed in the pathway at the end of the rows of vines in which each group works. As the grapes are picked, any that are damaged being first thrown to the ground, the pannier is held or placed directly beneath so that they tumble gently in with no loss of juice. Often fingertips, or a slight nudge with the closed tips of the secateurs are most effective at dislodging single withered grapes or small clusters of three or four; the secateur blades are useful when larger clusters must be clipped free from the bunch. The panniers are emptied into the *comportes* and, when these are filled, the dray is driven to the *chais* where the grapes are immediately crushed and pressed. Should it suddenly begin to rain, picking stops instantly, the panniers are hastily emptied into the *comportes*, the tarpaulin is thrown over them and, upon

arriving at the *chais*, the greatest care is taken to shuffle each *comporte*, beneath the tarpaulin, along the dray's floor to the entrance of the *chai*, lest droplets of rain should fall upon the grapes.

VINIFICATION

With the exception of the casks, the vinification equipment at Yquem has an antiquated charm and an aura of deeply entrenched tradition to which, one senses, Alexandre de Lur Saluces's sentimental attachment is much greater than that of Pierre Meslier. He delights

T*he pickers' lunch.*

Vigneronnes. *A cloud of botrytis spores rises*
as a vigneronne *empties her pannier into a* comporte.

As *the panniers are emptied into the* comportes,
the grapes are packed down.

in recounting the visits of the œnological and technological avant-garde, their horror at the venerable poverty of the equipment and, often, a downright refusal to believe that this is really what is used, or that it is physically possible for an estate the size of Yquem to make wine only with the help of these funny, little old machines. The answer, of course, is that relatively few grapes are ever pressed at Yquem in a single day: the entire wine production averages about one-fifth the amount expected of a Médoc first growth, and the *vendanges* last four to five times as long. There is, in fact, lurking in a far corner of the *chai*, a modern horizontal press,[20] identical to that in use at Château de Fargues,

whose presence might wrongly tempt an innocent visitor to suspect that these impeccably maintained, thickly varnished period objects are only museum show-pieces and that, behind the scenes, less glamorous equipment is put to use. The old equipment is irreplaceable, but it is nursed with a fanatical care that promises to keep it in use for many years to come. Each year, following the last pressing, all of the component parts are treated with a special, hard, alcohol-based varnish that, by now, forms a coat so thick that the definitions of contours, angles and joints are blurred like those of a culinary creation cloaked in aspic jelly.

A comporte *is emptied into the funnel of the crusher.*

A drayload of grapes at the
entrance to the vinification cellar (left-hand page).

A *basket filled with grapes is pushed on rails towards the press.*
Beginning of pressing. The wooden lid protects
the grapes from the metal surface of the hydraulic press.

Amidst a cloud of spores, a man stamps
the grapes in the basket while levelling them with a pitchfork
(left-hand page).

Built into the floor of the *chai* is a system of rails along which low, square, shallow-sided cars, designed to hold the upright stave baskets in which the grapes are pressed, may be moved easily back and forth between the *fouloir* (crusher), the three presses and the *émietteur* (crumbler).

The baskets. Each basket is formed of two semi-circular walls of spaced staves that lock together into an open cylinder, a solid wooden base the size of the outside circumference of the stave basket and a wooden lid measured to the inside circumference. When assembled, a thick woven straw mat the size of the lid is placed on the basket floor, and another is kept in readiness to be placed on top of the grapes before the lid is put on. Small wooden projections on the car floor keep the basket base slightly

elevated and a hole in one corner is kept plugged to prevent the loss of juice until it is intended to flow.

The crusher or fouloir. Installed on an elevated platform so that the basket may be placed beneath to receive the grapes, the *fouloir* or crusher is composed of a large wooden funnel within the base of which wooden, star-shaped rollers, fitting loosely into each other, are set in motion by an electrically operated belt. As the dray carrying the grapes arrives at the *chai*, its floor-level the same as that of the *fouloir* platform, two men hoist the *comportes*, one after the other, to the crusher and empty them in. Four drayloads, or fifty to sixty *comportes* of grapes, are needed to fill a basket (if the grapes arrive too slowly, it will be pressed partially filled), from which about two casks of must will be pressed.

The *fouloir* does not de-stalk; both grapes and stalk-fragments are churned through the rollers and spewed into the basket where a cellar-worker in rubber boots treads constantly,

Following the first pressing, the walls of the basket
are removed, revealing a dense cake of pomace which will be broken up
with a pitchfork and heaved into the émietteur, or crumbler. At the far end of
the émietteur a worker removes stalk fragments from the drum cage.

spreading the pulp with a pitchfork and stamping it into place to maintain a level surface.

When the basket is filled to the brim, the straw mat and the lid are placed on top, and it is moved into position beneath one of the presses. Hydraulic power lifts the car from its rails, moving it and the basket imperceptibly upwards to meet the stationary press. A pipe is attached to the outlet in the car floor, which is then unplugged, and the juices pass through a sieve to remove fragments of pulp before flowing into a glass-lined, 9,000-litre vat that is installed beneath the floor level. The violent flow of juices slowly reduces to a trickle, then to an irregular drip, and, one-and-a-half to two hours later, the dial registers 200 kilograms of pressure per square centimetre of surface, the contents of the basket are diminished by half and the first pressing is finished.

The crumbler or émietteur. Back on the rails, the car is wheeled to one end of the *émietteur*, or crumbler, an elongated wooden drum from whose inside walls project a pattern of jagged, enamelled metal teeth with an angle to their thrust that directs the whirling pomace in a spiralling path to the far end of the drum, which terminates in a latticed wooden cage through which the broken-up pressings, separated from their stemmy bits, are flung. A freshly prepared car and basket are positioned at this end to receive them.

The original basket is unlocked, its walls are removed with hook, chains and pulley (and immediately hosed down), and the lid and straw mat are removed to reveal a dense, almost impenetrable cake of pomice. As a worker digs in with a pitchfork, heaving chunks of pomice into one end of the *émietteur*, another worker, as before, treads, stamps and spreads the pressings in the new basket, while reaching from time to time into the semi-open end of the lattice drum cage to remove and discard the stalks which are collecting there.

The three pressings. The residue of two first-pressing baskets is required to fill a new basket for the second pressing. The grapes are pressed three times (in the past, the drained-dry pomace, or *marc*, served as compost in the vineyard – present legislation requires that it be sent off to a government distillery).

Whereas, with other white wines, the first pressing is always considered to give the finest wine and often is not mixed with succeeding pressings, the greatest extract and sugar concentration at Yquem are drawn from the second and third pressings. The grapes in the most extreme state of dehydration only give their juices the third time around. About 80 per cent of the juice is extracted in the first pressing, 15 per cent in the second and 5 per cent in the third; if the glucometer measures 19° potential alcohol in the juice of the first, that of the second will read about 21° and the third close to 25°.

The total amount of juice extracted from a day's picking can run the gamut of extremes: in some years never more than nine *barriques* are filled per day (in 1969, the smallest daily production was one barrel) and, in others, there may be as many as thirty-six; in 1976, this record was sustained daily throughout the height of the *vendange*, repeatedly imposing twenty-hour work days on the cellar-workers.

The barrels. The wine of each vintage begins its life in new oak, standard 225-litre *barriques bordelaises*, or hogsheads, the equivalent of 300 bottles. In these barrels it is fermented and raised, settling and clarifying progressively as it is transferred back and forth amongst the same barrels, until it is ready for bottling in the month of March three and a half years later (after bottling, some of these barrels will go to Château de Fargues and the remainder will be sold off to other vineyards).

For Yquem's purposes, the limited volume of the *barrique bordelaise* and the insulating nature of the wood provide the ideal fermenting vessel for a maximum proliferation of yeasts and a perfect temperature control, both especially important in the presence of naturally sluggish fermentations.

During its long sojourn in the casks, the wine must never be directly in contact with air but the wood's porosity, however slight, permits a minimal oxygenation which is beneficial to the wine's evolution. At the same time, an enrichening process takes place because of the slow evaporation through the pores of the wood : because the molecules of water are much smaller, they pass more readily through the dense oaken fibre than those of alcohol, despite the latter's greater volatility – thus, most of the loss is in the form of water, leaving in the wine a greater concentration of alcohol and the wine's other components.

By the time that it is ready for bottling, Yquem's wine, already vastly diminished thanks to limited production and to botrytis concentration, is further reduced in volume by something over 20 per cent through a combination of evaporation, finings (*collages* – the addition of a foreign substance, whisked into temporary suspension, that is either insoluble or is rendered insoluble by contact with certain elements in the wine's make-up,

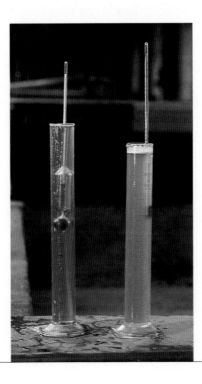

The must is measured in a glucometer (right) ; the beaker to the left has been filled with clear wine to show the form of the measuring instrument.

*The first-year cellar. The solid glass stoppers have replaced
the overturned half-bottles that permit the
escape of carbon dioxide gas during fermentation.*

and which possesses the faculty of attracting to it the pulverized particles of grape skins and pulp, dead yeast cells, unwelcome bacteria and other impurities in suspension in the wine, before precipitating, with the impurities in tow, to the bottom of the cask), and rackings (*soutirages* – the act of drawing the wine off one cask and putting it into another, leaving behind the lees, or deposit, which have settled to the bottom of the first cask, either through natural sedimentation or as a result of a preceding *collage*). This means that, on an average, some fifty barrels of Yquem will have been sacrificed to topping up (*ouillage*).

The barrels, made of the best oak available, especially chosen for Château d'Yquem, are furnished by Bordeaux coopers. Only oak from a continental climate, with sharply defined seasons and very cold winters, produces the tight-grained, knotless wood (from which the staves must be hand-split, never sawn) essential to a perfect cask. The bulk of it comes from the Limousin but, depending on the quality and the availability of the Limousin oak, it may be supplemented in some years by Slovenian oak from northern Yugoslavia.

The oak lends its own tannin and flavours to the wine and blasting the wood with flames, to permit bending the staves into their arched form, leaves a characteristic toasted taste. Only a wine with a powerful and complex structure and an imposing personality can support the superimposition of these extra seasoning agents, the new tannin merely underlining the wine's inherent force, the new flavours eventually integrating to create a single harmony. The oak's tannins also act as a clarifying agent upon the material in suspension in the wine, hastening its precipitation.

The barrels are delivered ready for use except for being rinsed in very hot water and drained ; those intended to be filled after the day's *vendange* are prepared in the morning. Each barrel is turned upside-down over a rotating keg rinser (*rince-fût rotatif*) which projects powerful jets of hot water into it as it is twirled. After being rolled, shaken and emptied, the barrels are placed, bung-hole-down, on elevated rails to drain before being installed on rails at ground level in the first-year cellar.

Fermentation. In Emile Peynaud's *Connaissance et travail du vin*, we read : " The mechanism of the fermentation of sugar is of a prodigious complexity. The schema of transformations involves no less than some thirty successive reactions, drawing into play a large number of enzymes. One might say that enzymes are a yeast's tools, each adapted to one of the steps in the transformation. Each reaction necessitates a specific tool, a different enzyme... "

Briefly, the fermentation of grape juice is a process by which yeasts, while feeding upon a small portion of the grape sugars and multiplying by the millions, produce enzymes that break down a large part of the remaining sugars into approximately equal parts of alcohol and of carbon-dioxide gas, which escapes into the air. A tiny fraction of the sugars are, at the same time, transformed into glycerol and a number of different elements.

Different yeasts are active at different stages of the fermentation : certain of them, particularly sensitive to alcohol, are responsible for launching the fermentation. During this early stage, they multiply rapidly but are paralysed or perish at relatively low alcohol levels ; then other yeasts take over the relay – one, in particular, *saccharomyces ellipsoideus*, is the commonest of the wine yeasts and especially active within a range of from 5° to 12° of alcohol; as these become increasingly sluggish in the presence of the rising alcohol level, another yeast *saccharomyces oviformis*, capable under certain circumstances of supporting up to 18° of alcohol, begins rapidly multiplying to finish the fermentation.

Dr Peynaud enumerates twenty-nine species of yeasts that are active during the vinification of different wines from the Bordelais region. Only a few have a pronounced effect on the fermentation, but it is impossible to know exactly what the subtle effects of the relatively inactive majority may be on the quality of the wine.

Over a period of decades or centuries, a process of natural selection and reproduction amongst the indigenous yeasts establishes a population both in the vineyard and in the *chais* that not only facilitates the fermentation process (fermentation is always less problematical in *chais* that have been in use for many years), but contributes to the definition of the specific personality of a wine.

The surface of a grapeskin presents a fantastic microfloral landscape; when it becomes host to noble rot, some of the original population is either altered or replaced by new elements. Amongst the latter is a yeast, smaller and more elongated than its invisible brethren, that exists only in the presence of noble rot; its name is *torulopsis bacillaris* and it is responsible for launching the fermentation of a Sauternes. It can resist levels of alcohol falling between 7° and 10° before the other yeasts take over in full force.

The Yquem balance. In dry wines the sugars are fermented out to the point where any remaining traces are imperceptible on the palate. The must of desiccated grapes, unaffected by noble rot, can be fermented to high degrees of alcohol before the alcohol renders the yeasts inactive, leaving a varying amount of residual sugar in the wine.

In the fermentation of musts affected by noble rot, the inhibiting action of the antibiotic botryticine arrests the fermentation at a level lower than the alcohol would have done in its absence. The precise level at which fermentation is arrested depends on the concentration of botryticine and, since the botryticine concentration and the concentration of the natural grape sugars work hand-in-hand, we are faced with what, on the surface, appears to be a contradiction: the greater the concentration of sugar, the lower the degree of alcohol; the lesser the concentration of sugar, the higher the degree of alcohol. It is by measuring the sugar level that we can estimate the point at which fermentation will be arrested and the resultant balance of alcohol and residual sugar in the finished wine. This is done with a glucometer or mustimeter (*pèse-moût*), a simple device by which a weighted, graduation-marked glass tube, thermometer-like in appearance, is immersed in a laboratory beaker containing grape juice, or must; the level at which it floats indicates the sugar content in terms of potential degrees of alcohol, or the percentage of alcohol that the sugar would be capable of producing if it were possible for it to be completely fermented out.

Beyond 35° potential alcohol, fermentation is practically impossible; at 25° potential alcohol, an intensely sweet wine will result with no more than 10° to 11° alcohol, whereas beneath a potential of 18° alcohol the wine becomes progressively drier and more alcoholic. About 20° potential alcohol is considered to produce the ideal real alcohol-residual sugar balance for a classic Château d'Yquem. With slight variations of from 19.8°

to 20.5° potential alcohol, the relation of real or acquired alcohol to residual sugar will vary from about 15° to 13.5° alcohol with from 4.8° to 7° – 80 to 120 grams (2 1/2 to 4 oz) per litre – of unfermented sugar remaining in the wine (by comparison, wines described as *demi-sec* retain about 20 grams [3/4 oz] of sugar per litre, *moelleux* or semi-sweet wines around 35 grams [1 oz] per litre). These figures are only theoretical and the fermentation may be arrested at a slightly lower or higher alcohol level for a given degree of potential alcohol. They do, however, give a dependable, general idea of what happens, on condition that all the sugars in the must issue from the grapes themselves, all, or for the most part, affected by noble rot – and, as Pierre Meslier notes, "on condition that the rot be noble".

The fermentations of these musts with high sugar and botryticine concentrations are always difficult; the rising level of alcohol and the presence of the botryticine, both powerful antiseptics, create an increasingly arid milieu for the multiplication of the yeasts. In explaining the torpid fermentations at Yquem, Pierre Meslier says, " Nos levures sont des petites vieilles, toutes ridées." ("Our yeasts are wrinkled little crones."). When a dab of must, unaffected by botrytis, is examined beneath the lens of a microscope, the *saccharomyces* yeasts are smooth, full and ovoid. The same yeasts from a Sauternes must, when compared with plump, ripe grapes, untouched by noble rot, seem to present a very exact analogy to the appearance of botrytis-withered grapes.

The viscid, sticky must, murky with a suspension of greyish-yellow silt, solid extractions from the grape skins and pulp, is pumped directly from the underground vat into the barrels in the first-year *chai*. The pre-fermentation racking, or *débourbage*[21] which requires the addition of a sulphurous solution to the juices, is out of the question at Yquem, both because the must's extraordinary density resists sedimentation and because botryticine is much more sensitive to sulphur dioxide than are the yeasts and would either be permanently impaired or eliminated by this treatment, destroying the delicate interplay of transformations that leads to a spontaneous fermentation arrest at the ideal alcohol-sugar balance.

The barrels are filled short of some ten or twelve litres to avoid the must's foaming up and overflowing as the fermentation approaches its tumultuous phase. An overturned, empty half-bottle is placed in each bunghole to prevent the entrance of air and, at the same time, to permit the release of carbon dioxide, the neck of the bottle insuring that it is not thrust to the floor by the pressure of the escaping gas. The fermentation begins almost immediately and a protective blanket of carbon dioxide rapidly forms within the cask, expelling the air. A distinctive, persistant buzzing sound fills the air; it has been likened to that of an apiary, to the cicadas on a July day in Provence, and to the "sound of the sea" in a conch shell. If one's ear is pressed against a cask, the buzz becomes a roar.

As soon as the tumultuous phase has peaked and the fermentation's activity begins to subside, the barrel is progressively topped up and will be filled to the brim by the time the fermentation is arrested. The half-bottles are replaced by the traditional heavy, solid glass stoppers which will shield the wine from contact with air for the remainder of its life in the wood.

The composition of the musts is different every day and, from each day's portion of

Barrels in the cellar.

barrels, a different wine is made. Each barrel is marked with the date of picking, and the potential alcohol reading and any other relevant information for that date will be noted in the cellar book so that an identity file for every barrel of wine is always at hand. It may be politic to cut and mix the contents of barrels from different days to equalize the musts, enlivening listless fermentations and imposing new identity files.

The eventual stability of the wine requires that the fermentation be conducted at close to 20° C (68° F), but the wine's finesse will suffer if the temperature rises much beyond

that figure. The fermentation in some barrels may be finished in as little as two weeks, others may require as long as six weeks. (Often the fermentation of the earlier *tries* is less phlegmatic than that of musts from later pickings, but there may also be variations from one barrel to another in a single day's batch.) Because of the extended *vendanges*, this means that the *chai* may be occupied by casks at varying stages of fermentation for up to three months or more, in part during the coldest weeks of the year. The *chai* must not only be heated until the entire process of fermentation is finished but, because of the escaping carbon dioxide gas, it must always be well aerated.

The barrels are rinsed with hot water.

RAISING THE WINE (l'élevage)

Topping up and racking (l'ouillage et le soutirage). As the fermentation draws to its close the wine begins to settle, the coarser and heavier substances falling out of suspension and collecting in the hollow of the cask's base. The wine is cloudy but stable, in the sense that no secondary fermentation will erupt to disorder its evolution (the malolactic fermentation, a deacidifying phenomenon that preoccupies makers of dry wines, is unknown to wines restructured by noble rot); its entire career in oak, from now on, is a question of progressive refinement and clarification. Until it is bottled, the casks will be topped up twice weekly – the barrels of wine used for this purpose being broken down and kept in smaller, hermetically closed or corked kegs, jugs or bottles.

As soon as the fermentation is finished, the wine is racked, racked again one month later and, henceforth, will be racked every three months – in all, fifteen rackings. Each time, the emptied barrel into which the wine will be racked is first sterilized, as a protective measure against oxidation and acetic bacterial infection, by a lighted sulphur wick being suspended inside from a wire attached at the bunghole.

Selection and assemblage. The definitive composition and balance of the vintage evolves over a period of some eighteen months. In the course of the first winter, regular tastings, supplemented by laboratory analyses, will permit Alexandre de Lur Saluces, Guy Latrille and Pierre Meslier to make a joint decision about which barrel will go into the *assemblage* for Château d'Yquem.

Every year a certain number of barrels are eliminated for, despite every effort, all of the *tries* cannot be equally successful; particularly, in years when rains precede the beginning or the end of the vintage, these early and late pickings often weigh in at low potential alcohol readings. In addition to this, the Sauvignon normally ferments out to about 15° real alcohol with mere traces of residual sugar and, for the taste balance, approximately 20 per cent of Sauvignon is necessary to the Yquem *assemblage*. This means that, for the ideal Sauvignon–Sémillon potential alcohol balance of 20° to be achieved, the overall average of the barrels of Sémillon, which may vary, individually, from as little as 16° to 25° or more, must be at least 21°.

If the bulk of the erratic Sauvignon's production is needed for the Yquem *assemblage* and if the barrels of Sémillion with low readings cannot be counter-balanced by barrels with unusually high readings, then these barrels, however perfect the wine by other standards, must be eliminated. On condition that an excess of Sauvignon will permit an *assemblage* of " Y ",[22] the ideal solution is to channel these light Sémillons in that direction. Inevitably, in the best of years, at least 10 per cent of the harvest is disposed of anonymously to be raised by the buyers and used in shippers' blends of generic Sauternes or Bordeaux A.O.C.

The *assemblage* begins in the spring following the vintage and continues progressively, in stages, throughout the following year, forty barrels at a time being racked into the same vat used at the time of pressing before being pumped back into the sterilized barrels. Because this operation involves more contact with air than a normal cask-to-cask racking, a light dose of sulphurous solution is added to the vat before the wine is returned to the casks.

The ouillage *(topping up).* The soutirage *(racking).*

*While topping up, the flow of wine from
the pouring spout is stopped at the instant the barrel is filled to
the level of the bunghole (right-hand page).*

Fining. The shock of seasonal changes in temperature effects a natural sedimentation in the wine but, for a wine of Yquem's texture and density (1.045 as opposed to .992 for a dry white wine, assuming the density of water to be 1.000 or a weight of 1,000 grams per litre), fining is none the less indispensable to its brilliance. Without this process the light, powdery suspensions cannot be precipitated out, their own weight being often no greater than that of the wine, while even heavier material, if very fine, is prevented from depositing by the wine's viscous textural resistance.

The wine is fined during its second winter. Depending on the vintage's aptitude for self-clarification, it may or may not be fined again a year later.

The wine is more or less receptive to different precipitating mediums from one year to another. The substances used are gelatine, albumin and bentonite (a colloidal clay from the western United States). Each year experiments are made in the laboratory with half-bottles of wine and these fining agents to determine which of them, singly or in combination and in what proportions, will be most effective for the vintage. The quantity of fining agent required for a correct *flocculation* also varies with the year and with the choice of agents, but it is always a small amount.

A special whisk, with propeller-like blades that open up inside the cask when put into motion, is used to instantly disperse the fining agent, added in solution, throughout the mass of wine, which is then left *sur colle*, or " on its finer ", for two or three weeks before being racked.

THE BOTTLING PROCESS

The wine is bottled in the month of March in its fourth year. It is first racked, twenty casks at a time, into a wooden vat installed at a height permitting the wine to flow by gravitational force. On its path from the vat to the bottles, it passes through a fine sieve which eliminates any trace of sediment.

The bottles are filled and corked mechanically ; as each leaves the bottling line, it is examined with a magnifying glass to ascertain that the cork is in perfect condition and that an accident in corking will not have caused a shard of torn cork to be let loose in the wine. The bottles are dressed with labels and capsules and wrapped in tissue by hand.

A relatively small portion of each year's production is put into magnums and half-bottles ; the demand for half-bottles by far exceeds their distribution, through no fault of Yquem's but because, until recently, the Bordeaux shippers have refused more than a token number. They are " re-examining the situation ", however, and, in years to come, there will certainly be more half-bottles on the market. (It is true that half-bottles age more rapidly than bottles – and that magnums age more slowly – but when one realizes that 70- and 80-year-old halves of Yquem are presently in perfect condition, one need entertain no disquietude for the future of today's half-bottles.)

Ideally, the wine should now be tucked away on its side in a perfect cellar – silent and without reverberations, moderately humid, decently aerated, never far from 12° C (53°-54° F) – and forgotten for half a life-time. Once it leaves the estate, the people who have nursed it until now have no more control ; as a final precaution against its suffering from the insolence of careless shippers, long hot or cold ocean voyages and the extremes of temperature in warehouses the world over, the bottles are first wrapped individually in thick insulating paper sleeves filled with a fine julienne of wood shavings before being packed into larger-than-normal wooden cases. This provides only a partial protection ; merchants who willingly accept the extra expense of shipping in climatized containers deserve applause and gratitude.

TWO CENTURIES AGO

Two centuries ago, the methods of vinification and *élevage* were empirical, evolved through experience and observation. Superimposed upon these traditions today is a body of scientific explanation, the knowledge not only of what happens but of why and how things happen. Yet, at least at Yquem, not much has changed : the grapes were picked in *tries*, the wine was fermented in *barriques*, it was regularly topped up, racked and fined, and a sulphur wick was always burnt in the barrels at the time of racking.

Wine was sold either bottled at the château or in barrels. A ledger entry from the Yquem archives reads, " Le 25 février 1791. tiré 2 Bques en bouteilles, qui étoient sur le fouet depuis le 8 dudit. il y en a eu 554 bouteilles, dont 500 ont été Expédiées le 25 fév. en 10 caisses à M. Jefferson ... " (" 25 February 1791. drew 2 *barriques* into bottles, which had been " on the whip " since the 8th of the month. there were 554 bottles, of which 500 were shipped the 25 Feb. in 10 cases to Mr Jefferson ... "). A wine that was *sur le fouet* had been whisked, that is to say, fined, but not racked. Nowhere is the choice of fining agent mentioned, but it was customary at that time to use isinglass, or fish gelatine, still very much in use today (its properties are somewhat different from those of gelatine drawn from hooves and bones) for white wines, and egg whites for reds. It would be hard to say whether the *barriques* were slightly smaller or the bottles slightly larger than those in use today ; efforts had been made since the sixteenth century to standardize the *barrique bordelaise* by imposing outside measures, but the precise volume of 225 litres was not standardized until 1858.

An undated document (probably 1804, since it suggested that the 1801 vintage might be ready for bottling or might require another six months in barrels), apparently a draft for a letter (lines are crossed out and rewritten) to a client concerning the care of barrels of wine delivered to him, is remarkable for its precision of detail and the similarity of all the operations to the treatment of wine at Yquem today. Although it is not stated, the insistence on the time of racking suggests that the wine had been fined just before delivery. The client was probably a merchant as the breaking down of a *barrique* for topping up suggests a large number of barrels – in shipments of only two or three casks, recorded elsewhere in the cellar books, cases of bottled wine accompanied them for *ouillage*. *Tirage au fin* was the term then used for *soutirage*, or racking ; Dutch matches was the term for sulphur wicks :

Le vin blanc de 1801 du cru d'Yquem haut Sauterne expédié à Monsieur Kabanac devra être ouillé en arrivant à sa destination ; on le tiendra plein, on le laissera, ainsi, reposé pendant une quinzaine de jours ou trois semaines ; on le tirera ensuite au fin par un beau temps et un vent du nord, s'il est possible ; pour cela on emploiera, pour tirer la 1ʳᵉ, une bonne barrique en vidange

119

*Guy Latrille, the cellar master,
pours wine from a pipette, into a glass for tasting,*

120

then scents the second-year Yquem. The glass stopper is replaced.

blanche, et fraîche dans laquelle on fera brûler, après avoir été bien rincée avec deux ou 3 eaux fines, environ 3 pouces de bonnes allumettes de hollande ; on en usera de même pour les barriques suivantes après avoir laissé tomber le peu de lie qui s'y trouvera ; on le laissera reposer 12 ou 15 jours, on le goutera alors, et si on le trouve trop jeune pour être mis en bouteilles, on l'attendra 5 ou 6 mois en ayant soin de le tirer au fin 2 fois dans cet intervalle en observant les mêmes précautions que dessus pour le tirage et pour qu'il soit toujours plein ; comme il est essentiel qu'il soit ouillé du même vin, on fera bien de commencer à en défaire une barrique pour cela, et pour le remplacement de la lie (après soutirage) et du vin (perdu par évaporation) ; il suffira de mettre 2 pouces d'allumettes dans ces deux derniers tirages au lieu de 3, et on aura l'attention de ne pas la laisser trop brûler, pour qu'il ne tombe pas de linge brûlé dans la barrique ; après le soufre brûlé, on tournera la barrique pour la laisser égoutter par la bonde.

" The 1801 white wine from the growth of Yquem haut Sauterne shipped to Monsieur Kabanac should be topped up on arriving at its destination ; it should be kept full, it should be left, thus, to settle for fifteen days or three weeks ; then one should draw it off completely during fine weather and a north wind, if possible ; to do so one should use, to draw off the first one, a good, freshly emptied cask in which will be burnt, after it has been well rinsed 2 or 3 times with clear water, about 3 inches of good Dutch matches ; one should use it in the same way for the following casks after having drained off the small amount of lees that they contain ; it should be left to rest for 12 or 15 days, then tasted, and if it is found to be too young for bottling, one should wait 5 or 6 months, taking care to draw it off 2 times during this interval while observing the same precautions as above for drawing it off and for keeping it always full ; since it is essential that it always be topped up with the same wine, one will do well to begin by breaking down a barrel for this purpose, both for replacing the lees (after racking) and the wine (lost through evaporation) ; it is enough to use 2 inches of matches for these last two rackings instead of 3, and one should take care not to let it burn too much, lest some burnt cloth fall into the barrel ; after the sulphur is burned, one should turn the barrel upside down and leave it to drain by the bunghole. "

Then, as now, March was considered an ideal time for bottling because of cool weather, winds and generally high barometer readings ; elsewhere, it was noted that the wines are clearest in March.

The age at which the wine was bottled was a function of when it was sold ; for instance, the cellar book entries for the first week of January 1817 record rackings of 1802, 1805, 1807 and 1811, some as a preparation to being shipped, either in casks or in bottles, and others as a matter of course. The wine was kept, not only in *barriques*, but in *futailles* (quarter-*barriques*), *double futailles* (half-*barriques*), *pièces* (containing five *barriques*) and *foudres* (5 or 10,000 litres). There are no indications that young wines were kept in anything but standard *barriques* and, as the supply of older wines began to grow short, they had to be drawn back into *pièces* from *foudres*, and into *barriques* from *pièces*. As supplies of a vintage grew short, it sometimes had to be topped up with the wine of another vintage. Thus, an entry, also from January 1817, reads : " Drew off foudre no. 11 1805 wine five *barriques* and replaced them with what follows *To Wit* : 2 1/2 *barriques* 1805 ; 1 *barrique* 1807 ; 1 1/2 *barriques* 1811 ; Put into *double futailles* the five barriques taken from the *foudre.*" And again 12 January 1812 reads : " Emptied *pièce* no. 6 1806 wine. Drew off 5 1/2 *barriques*. Drew a little off each *barrique* to finish filling the 6th barrique. Topped up with 1809 wine ... ".

The use of the large 1,125-litre (approximately) barrels and the huge tuns was not only a space-saver but, for wines that were kept for so long before bottling, extremely practical, for ageing is greatly slowed down in larger vessels. The shifting back and forth from *barrique* to *foudre* to *pièce* to *barrique* served also as an equalizing influence in the same way as today's more precisely organized *assemblages*.

" He poured himself a glass of Château d'Yquem ... Kallomeïtsef
did the same and swore by the great gods that the wine was exquisite "
Turgenev
Virgin Soil

The bottles are dressed and crated.

*Each bottle is examined with a magnifying glass
to ensure its perfect condition.*

YQUEM
AND THE TABLE

Some claim that Yquem should not be marred by the proximity of food; others sip it on a virgin palate while nibbling a peach. It is obvious that a clinical analysis of any wine is best performed in the morning, when one's nose and tastebuds are freshest, and without the distraction of competing scents and savours, however pleasantly they may mingle with those of the wine. But, although it is possible to consider an Yquem as a solitary work of art, just as a preparation of disparate ingredients conjured by culinary magic into a unit of harmonious accents may be admired out of the context of a menu, neither one nor the other, alone, can afford the same intensity of pleasure or satisfaction. Both the ritual of form and the shifting levels of interplay amongst the wines and the foods are vital to the highest expression of the individual elements and to that of the larger picture.

A progression of wines and foods forms a network of inter-relationships whose success depends upon each wine and its accompanying dish mutually enhancing the other, while the play amongst the dishes expands in dramatic form, each thrown into relief by the one preceding it as it performs the same service for the one to follow. To complete the picture, there is usually a mounting drama amongst the wines from young, light-bodied and delicate to progressively older and more complex or, perhaps, lighter to bigger and denser vintages and greater distinction of origins. This is where one runs into trouble with a Sauternes, the more so with an Yquem: light-bodied it is not, and its vibrant intensity grips the palate as do few other wines – in the wake of an Yquem, most suffer badly. An obvious solution is to place it in glorious apotheosis, after all the other wines, on a cautiously chosen dessert, on fresh fruit – or by itself.

When opening a meal with Sauternes, a double consommé, served between it and the wine to follow, is a very effective palate restorer. Or, a sturdy red wine with the jubilant fruit and the rough edges of youth may be able to support the Sauternes' precedence with no transitional interlude, preparing the way for other reds that require more pampering : a dark, tannic Graves or Médoc, served cool, too young for drinking under other circumstances, will work and so will a young Côte-Rôtie, Cornas or Hermitage (the dense, inky fruit of these last wines will probably require older ones from the same region to follow).

Menus at Château d'Yquem are often built around a suite of four or five Sauternes. Foie gras, whose marriage with Sauternes has finally been consecrated by wide experience and acceptance, usually opens. If turbot, brill or sole, in a creamy sauce, or a gratin of crayfish tails follows, mallard or other game birds – often with an unsweetened fruit garnish – or roast guinea fowl or chicken may succeed it ; if the fish is a simply grilled shad or bass, poultry may be served in a cream sauce or in a Sauternes-flavoured velouté. Roquefort, a destroyer of most wines, which Yquem supports with equanimity, is the star of the cheese platter and a discreetly sweetened pithiviers or other almond pastry often finishes.

The intention is not so much to launch a fashion in all-Sauternes repasts (for, while such a meal is a passionate experience, it tends to leave the diner breathless) as to instruct. The menus are " crash courses " in Sauternes food alliances and menu construction which teach that, not only may one serve a series of Sauternes with a meal but that, by extension, Sauternes can open and close a meal with other wines served between, or that it is possible to open with a red wine – or with a dry white followed by a red – and finish with two or three Sauternes on a main course, cheeses and dessert.

MENUS OF THE PAST

The problem of transition from a Sauternes to red wines seems never to have troubled our gastronomic forebears. Except for the progressive trimming of the number of dishes within each category in the menu, and a continuing simplification of presentations, the basic structure of a formal dinner menu, throughout the nineteenth century and until after the First World War, hardly budged. Yquem's place was always on a noble fish (turbot, brill, sole, salmon trout, or salmon), followed by red Bordeaux, then red Burgundies (in the Bordelais, the latter were sacrificed to a succession of Bordeaux) : the principle was lesser Bordeaux and lesser Burgundies with the braised meats and other entrées, followed by great growths, in the same order, with the roast birds, cold dishes and vegetables, but this rule was rarely respected to the letter. No cheeses were served and, without exception, Champagne was served from the moment the vegetables were removed until one left the table ; at no time before the 1920s was Sauternes thought of, or utilized as, a " dessert wine " – it would be out of place, here, to bemoan the fate of Champagne. Foie gras or other cold terrines, pâtés, galantines or mousses, cold langouste or lobster, dressed *en Bellevue*, chaud-froid preparations and composed salads, all of which, today, would be considered ideal starters upon which to place an Yquem, were buried deep in the menu after the meats or, if sorbets separated the entrées from the roasts, foie gras might follow the first, langouste and salad the second. Soups and sorbets were eliminated from lunches, but the tenets were otherwise the same.

Lest it be imagined that members of a certain level of society were subjected twice daily to this style of force-feeding, consider Brillart-Savarin's homely lunch for three, which he served in 1801 and, twenty-four years later, still apparently thought worthy of immortalizing in print : oysters washed down with two bottles of " Sauterne " – the other wines are not recorded ; skewered, grilled kidneys ; truffled foie gras ; *fondue* (eggs scrambled with cheese) ; fresh and preserved fruits.

To illustrate briefly recent menu evolution and Yquem's position therein, the " Dîner des Trois Empereurs " is a good starting-point. Earlier menus are more complicated and, although Yquem is preceded only by the Madeira or other fortified wines that followed the soups (an innovation of Talleyrand's, according to Brillat-Savarin), the logic of the wine service, in general, is difficult to grasp.

At one time, " Château-Yquem " or " Château Yquem " could as often be seen on menus as " Château d'Yquem " ; today the latter usage is consecrated, unless one simply writes " Yquem ".

7 June 1867

Impératrice, Fontanges	Canetons à la rouennaise	Madère retour des Indes 1846
Soufflé à la reine	Ortolans sur canapés	Xérès 1821
Filets de sole à la vénitienne	Aubergines à l'espagnole	Château Yquem 1847
Escalopes de turbot au gratin	Asperges en branches	Chambertin 1846
Selle de mouton purée bretonne	Cassolettes Princesse	Château Margaux 1846
Poulets à la portugaise	Bombe glacée	Château Latour 1847
Pâté chaud de cailles	Dessert	Château Lafite 1848
Homard à la parisienne		
Sorbets		

(Dinner of the three Emperors, at the Café Anglais,
Paris, 7 June 1867)

□ □ □

The Café Anglais was created in 1802 – a victim of demolition in 1913, the Tour d'Argent inherited the contents of its cellars. The chef Dugléré was at the height of his career ; the three emperors were the tsar Alexander II, the future Alexander III and the king of Prussia. The 1847 Yquem is the same for which, eight years earlier, the tsar's brother, the grand duke Constantine, had paid a record price.

Hardly typical for any period, the following celebrated menu, served in La Salle des Pressoirs at Château d'Yquem to 200 French and foreign journalists and celebrities, was one of the events in a promotional campaign organized by the proprietors of Yquem, Haut-Brion, Margaux, Latour, Lafite and Mouton, in celebration of their mutual decision to release only château-bottled wines (years later, the marquis de Lur Saluces observed that forty was the absolute maximum number of guests that it was possible to receive at Yquem).

At Lafite, the preceding day, the marquis had presided at a lunch for the same 200 guests on which the wines from the other châteaux had been placed with a Lafite 1811, the legendary "year of the comet", in the star position. The following year, Le Groupe des Six again received guests, in the same spirit, but this time at a dinner organized at the " Pré-Catelan " in the Bois de Boulogne which wound up with an Yquem 1900, sagely accompanied by fruit.

Château d'Yquem, 14 June 1926
(From *Le Grand Livre de la cuisine*, by Prosper Montagné and Prosper Salles)

Consommé en tasses	Château Filhot 1904
Langouste a la Sévigné	Château Yquem 1914
Aiguillettes de caneton à l'orange	Château Yquem 1921
Filet froid servi à la façon du Périgord	Château Yquem 1869
Asperges nouvelles	
Salade de saison	
Parfait Trianon	
Desserts	

*Lunch for 200 French and foreign journalists
given by the proprietors of the* grands crus *on 14 June 1926,
in the* salle des pressoirs *at château d'Yquem,
prepared by M. Chézeau* traiteur *in Bordeaux.*

□ □ □

Here is a pre-First World War festive family menu (from Yquem's archives), a brilliant example of the classic formula pared to the naked essentials, a style that we might do well to revive.

23 October 1913
Mademoiselle Marguerite Duret

Potage Sévigné	Xérès
Timbales financière	Château Yquem 1908
Turbot sauce mousseline	Château Latour 1881
Lièvre à la royale	Château Haut-Bailly 1895
Médaillons de ris châtelaine	Château Petit-Village 1895
Pintadeaux aux truffes	Château Haut-Brion (Magnum) 1896
Foie gras en Bellevue	Château Mouton-Rothschild 1870
Salade gauloise	Champagne Delbeck
Glace Marie-Louise	
Desserts	

□ □ □

The menu below, for a dinner at which guests wore costumes from the year 1900, was organized by Madeleine Decure who, with Curnonsky, was co-founder of *Cuisine et Vins de France,* and Alex Allégrier, proprietor of Lucas-Carton. No other restaurant in Paris could have lent itself as well as Lucas-Carton's nineteenth-century, pure " modern style " dining-room to the spirit of the evening. The costumes were extraordinary : one normally sedate and distinguished gentleman of a certain age arrived with flaming red hair and a highly rouged visage in the guise of a mad duchess ; Madeleine Decure was a cameo from *A l'ombre des jeunes filles en fleurs* and Odette Kahn could have been taken for Swann's Odette.

In the year 1963 it was thought too foolhardy to carry authenticity to the point of shifting the Yquem to the salmon and throwing the Champagne onto the dessert – and the roast birds were missing to complete the classic formula. The menu and the service, none the less, succeeded in recapturing an aura of time past.

21 March 1963
Restaurant Lucas-Carton
Cercle des amis de " Cuisine et Vins de France "
Dîner travesti 1900

Consommé viveur aux paillettes d'or	Champagne Taittinger brut 1959
Saumon de Loire sauce Nantua	Puligny-Montrachet Clos de la Garenne 1961
Baron d'agneau de Pauillac bouquetière	en magnum (Joseph Drouhin à Beaune)
Neige comtes de Champagne	Château Bouscaut 1955 en magnum
Terrine de bécasses Brillat-Savarin	Graves rouges - Cru classé
Salade Mireille	(Victor Place à Cadaujac)
Fromages	La Tâche 1952 en magnum
Biscuit glacé Néluska	(Domaine de la Romanée-Conti)
Mignardises	Château Figeac 1950 en double magnum
	Saint-Émilion - 1er grand cru classé
	(M. Manoncourt)
	Château d'Yquem 1955 en magnum
	Sauternes - 1er grand cru classé
	(Marquis de Lur Saluces)
	Grande fine Champagne
	1er grand cru de Cognac
	(Marcel Ragnaud à Ambleville)

□　□　□

The following menu was conceived by Alice Waters and Jeremiah Tower, both intrepid and imaginative cooks with unusual talents. The following description by Alice Waters is taken from *The Chez Panisse Menu Cookbook* : " Jeremiah Tower's brilliant pairing of the entrecôte of beef with the Château d'Yquem resulted in a combination that married in an indescribably wonderful manner. And the sensation created by pairing the saltiness of the ham with the clean, light flavours of the Barsac, Château Caillou, was not one of overwhelming sweetness, but a perfectly balanced harmony.

" The entire concept of a meal with which one drinks Sauternes throughout is revolutionary in concept, but magnificent in effect. "

An American Menu
Restaurant Chez Panisse, Berkeley, California, 19 June 1975
A Sauternes Dinner

Culpepper, Virginia ham braised in	Château Caillou 1947
Sauternes and served with prunes stuffed	Château Climens 1949
with green olives	Château Doisy-Daëne 1949
Quenelles of salmon	Château d'Yquem 1955, 1967
with crayfish butter sauce	Château Guiraud 1959
Entrecôte of beef served with potatoes cooked	Château Suduiraut 1959
in butter and duck fat with mushrooms	Château d'Yquem 1922
Green apples filled with berries	
and served with crème fraîche	
Hot deep-dish fruit pie	
Almond cream dessert	
Caramelized walnuts and coffee	

□ □ □

Le Taillevent – Paris
27 May 1976

Consommé aux écrevisses en gelée	Champagne Krug 1966 en magnum
Cervelas de fruits de mer aux pistaches	Beaune Clos des Mouches 1973 Domaine Joseph Drouhin
Truffe sous pâte Taillevent	Château Haut-Batailley Pauillac 1971
Aiguillettes de caneton	Château Cheval-Blanc Saint-Émilion 1964 en magnum
au vin de Saint-Émilion	Château Lafite-Rothschild Pauillac 1961
Fromages de France	Château d'Yquem Sauternes 1967
Crêpes soufflées aux amandes	Café
	Liqueurs de France

The menu was conceived by Richard Olney
and prepared by Claude Deligne

□ □ □

The soufflé base for the crêpes was made of almond milk and garnished with split fresh almonds. A light, playful thing of great delicacy which provided a perfect framework for the illumination of Yquem's subtle tonalities and depth.

12 February 1984
Solliès-Toucas

Soupe de baudrois au safran	Apéritif : Krug 1976
Gigot, estouffade aux truffes	Anjou 1928
Fromages	Haut-Brion 1971
Crêpes aux pommes	Mouton 1953
	Léoville-Poyferré 1900
	Yquem 1937

The menu was conceived by Richard Olney

□ □ □

The crêpes are tender. The batter is made with more egg and less flour than most, a pinch of salt, no sugar, milk, a goodly amount of melted butter and a bit of Cognac. The apples are a variety of russet, *reinettes clochard*, unsightly but relatively non-acid; they are sliced and sautéed in butter with neither sugar nor seasoning, rolled in the crêpes, placed flap-side down, side-by-side, touching, in a buttered gratin dish, sprinkled lightly with sugar, dabbed with butter and put into a hot oven for about ten minutes or until hot and glazed.

Le Taillevent – Paris
Monday, 15 July 1985
" Grand dîner Yquem "
Organised by Bipin R. Desai and Richard Olney

Consommé de crustacés en gelée	Krug grande cuvée
Turbot braisé, sauce au Sauternes	Château d'Yquem 1945
Ragoût de ris de veau, de truffes,	Château d'Yquem 1937
de foie gras et de crêtes de coq	Château d'Yquem 1921
Granité de melon charentais au champagne	Château d'Yquem 1980
Caneton à l'aigre-doux	Château d'Yquem 1893
Fromages persillés	Krug 1979
Blanc-manger	pour vous rafraîchir le palais entre chaque plat

□ □ □

It is a nearly impossible task to build a menu successfully around a series of old Yquems – limited, furthermore, to the most famous and fabulous of vintages – each of which, under normal circumstances, merits the ultimate position in a wine service; the 1980 was placed on the cheeses to lend relief to the suite of old wines.

PARTICULAR AFFINITIES

Two conditions are fundamental to a successful matching of wine and food. The first concerns the wine service: the glasses must be sparkling and odourless; always smell them before use – in the best-kept of cupboards, if not used daily, they can rapidly acquire a musty odour that deforms the wine. The size and shape of the glass, when filled by somewhat less than half, should permit the wine to be easily swirled, its bouquet captured in the upper part of the glass's bowl; tulips are commonly used for Sauternes. But these precautions are useless if, at the moment of serving, the wine's temperature is not impeccable.

The perfect temperature of a given wine can vary with its age and, to some extent, with the seasons – the same wine served at the same temperature will seem cooler on the palate in summer than in winter. A young Sauternes can support a lower temperature than a fully mature one can but, iced, both will be paralysed with their nuance, complexity and depth shattered; if too warm, the wine's unity or balance is dispelled with alcohol, acids and sugars falling out of harmony. Personal taste may play a limited role, for between the temperatures of 8° C (46° F) and 12° C (54° F) the qualities of the wine may still be appreciated by the fiercest of temperature extremists – it should not be forgotten that a wine poured at 8° C will almost certainly have reached 10° C in the glass before it touches one's lips.

Secondly, in the kitchen, one must be supple. Respecting printed recipes will never do; the same dish often demands to be seasoned differently depending on the wine that has been chosen to accompany it. Recipes can be sources of inspiration and valuable points of departure – the best are those that describe briefly the principles of a dish and leave the details of the execution to the wit of the practitioner. Contrasts often form striking marriages but, at times, Sauternes also likes to find muted echos of itself in the food that it escorts – sensuous creamy textures, hints of sweetness or bitterness, memories of honey, almonds, peaches, – or of the indescribable nervous quality, a sort of vibrating high-strung tension, that is particular to Sauternes and that, even in small doses, transmits itself intact to a sauce.

If Sauternes is to be associated with a dish whose printed formula imposes another wine, if can often advantageously replace that wine, particularly when, in combination with fumet, stock or demi-glace, fish or white meats are braised in a small amount of liquid which is then transformed into a sauce. Good food can never be produced with wine of indifferent quality, but a good Sauternes that you would not be ashamed to serve at table will do very well in the kitchen and Yquem will accompany the finished dish to perfection.

The ancient amber Yquems are not the most versatile of Sauternes on a menu; with the most discreet of desserts, they will blossom in glory, yet they support even less sweetness than a younger Sauternes, say from five to twenty years old, which is also easier to associate with savoury preparations. Because excessive sweetness is rarely a problem with courses in the main body of the meal, the arena of choice is greater; it is imperative, whatever the age of the Sauternes, that its accompanying dessert be noticeably less sweet than the wine itself. Chocolate, red acidic fruits, ices and ice-creams are quarrelsome in the presence of Sauternes.

To discover new – or forgotten – alliances, one must systematically brush aside the old clichés, the intellectualizing, theorizing prejudices that evolve in a vacuum, out of contact

*Thérèse, who serves the informal meals in the
château's dining-room.*

with the real world of tasting and common sense. Tradition is unrelentingly stubborn (even though it lurches from one prejudice to another, which often contradict each other, as the past and present uses of Sauternes will bear witness) and the breakers of tradition are too often unrelentingly capricious in their destructive efforts. You have only your palate upon which to depend.

DISHES TO ACCOMPANY CHÂTEAU D'YQUEM

The liquorous, spicy bitterness of a Sauternes used in the preparation of a dish calls for a Sauternes accompaniment. There are also many dishes, in the confection of which no wine is used, whose savours, often with notes of sweetness, reflect the scents of Yquem, thrusting the wine into relief. The texture of the food is of no less importance. The velvety caress bestowed upon a dish by an egg-yolk liaison complements the voluptuous body of an Yquem.

Sweet or savoury custards : a rustic bread-and-butter pudding, for instance – lightly toasted, buttered slices of bread or brioche, laid in a buttered oven dish, over which is poured a mixture of 6 or 7 eggs, first whisked with sugar, then with half a bottle of Sauternes and half as much cream, baked in a bain-marie in a slow oven for an hour or until the centre is no longer liquid.

Sweet or savoury soufflés or crêpes soufflés : a spoonful of soufflé mixture placed off-centre on each crêpe, the other side folded loosely over the mixture, arranged on a buttered baking sheet, brushed with melted butter and, for a dessert, sprinkled with sugar, then baked in a hot oven for a few minutes or until swelled up ; or tapioca, semolina or vermicelli puddings mounted, like soufflés, with beaten egg whites, unmoulded and served warm with apricot or sabayon sauce (they are all classics ; check Escoffier).

A sabayon : made from a very old Sauternes, still lovely to drink but with its vitality beginning to slip, a sabayon will give a thrust of renewed vigour and youth to the old wine for its final curtain call – about 4 egg yolks to 100 g (4 oz, 1/2 cup) of sugar and 20 cl (6-7 fl oz) of wine ; whisk constantly in a bain-marie in progressively heating water, kept beneath the boil, until thickened and foamy, continuing to whisk for a minute after removing from the bain-marie ; if served cold, whipped cream may be incorporated into it. With a younger Sauternes, a savoury sabayon can be prepared in the same way for fish, braised or poached in a minimum of liquid, by eliminating the sugar and substituting a syrupy reduction of the cooking juices for part of the Sauternes.

Fruits

Apples : the flavour is enriched and the flat edge of sweetness is cut by cooking apples in butter, whether for a dessert or for a savoury garnish ; for the latter, the presentation is more attractive if they are grilled instead of being sautéed. Peel and core them, cut them into thick rounds, brush all over with melted butter, arrange them on a baking tray and grill them beneath a heat source or in an oven with both overhead and underneath heat until the surface is golden brown and they are lightly swelled. Don't try to turn them ; transfer them directly, with a spatula, to a heated serving platter or individual plates.

Apple mousses, puddings, pies, tourtes and tarts are all good Sauternes desserts : sauté sliced apples in butter until lightly caramelized, scatter them into a blind-baked pastry shell, pour over a whisked mixture of eggs, sugar, a pinch of powdered cinnamon and cream, bake until the cream is set, the pastry crisp and golden, and serve warm.

Fritters: apple rings, cut more thinly than for the savoury garnish, macerated with a sprinkling of sugar and eau-de-vie, dipped in batter, deep-fried and served hot, lightly dusted with icing sugar; pear rings or pitted and halved apricots are treated identically.

Pears: more often sweet than savoury but worth trying, sliced, in combination with brains or sweetbreads, in salads seasoned with lemon and cream or as a butter-cooked garnish for pork and game dishes. As a dessert, peeled, halved and cored, sliced and spread in a buttered gratin dish, sprinkled with sugar and eau-de-vie de poire, covered with the same mixture that was used for the apple tart, baked and served warm.

Pears poached in red wine are good with Sauternes or treat them as follows: peel, halve and core the pears and arrange tightly in a star pattern, cut surface up, in a copper frying pan, round gratin dish or tatin mould, with a fragment of cinnamon bark, a sprinkling of sugar and a bottle of red wine poured over. Bring to the boil and simmer, covered, for an hour or so; with the lid held on, drain off the wine, reduce it to a thick syrup and pour it back over the rearranged pears in their pan; cover loosely with a round of short paste or rough puff and bake for 40 minutes or until the pastry is golden and crisp. It is best served warm and, in any case, unmoulded – the glistening deep purple star of pear mounds facing up – only at the moment of serving to prevent the juices from soaking into the pastry; thick or whipped cream on the side, if liked, but altogether unnecessary.

Peaches: like pears, poached in red wine, peeled but left whole, unpitted, for the beauty of the thing; wine reduced to a light syrup and poured back over the peaches, preferably in a crystal bowl, to cool. The best dessert in the world is a bowl filled with peeled and sliced (richly flavoured and fully ripe, but not bruised with brown spots) yellow peaches, sprinkled with sugar, a bottle of fifty-year-old (forty or sixty...) Sauternes poured over, the bowl tightly covered over with plastic film-wrap and refrigerated for an hour or so while the flavours intermingle; pour over, for instance, a 1937 first growth and serve at the same time an old Yquem. White peaches are a completely different fruit, also lovely in Sauternes but better suited to being immersed in one that is still confined within the steely contours of its youth.

Figs (tree-ripened): summer figs cannot compare with the deep-red-fleshed, green- or purple-black-skinned autumn varieties. As an opener, *à l'Italienne*, accompanied by raw ham (for a variation, see " Salads " below); as a dessert, peeled, a cross cut half-way down, pressed half-open, sprinkled with sugar and Sauternes and warmed in the oven – dabs of cream can be placed on top; as garnish to roast or braised pork, duck, wild rabbit, etc., they should only be heated briefly, sprinkled or not with a sauce, at the last minute to avoid their disintegrating during cooking.

Dried figs: simmer dried figs in red wine with a couple of sprigs of thyme and 2 or 3 tablespoons of honey for an hour or so – delicious either warm or cold. For a dessert at least as good and more presentable, strain off all the wine and reduce it to a thick syrup, loosened just before removing it from the heat with a dash of Chartreuse; halve the figs, sprinkle over a few drops of green Chartreuse, roll them in crêpes, arrange in a buttered gratin dish, spoon over the syrup, place a thin strip of butter on each crêpe and reheat, until the juice is bubbling, in a hot oven.

Almonds and pistachios : to peel, plunge them into boiling water for a few seconds, drain and rub them briskly between towels ; most will be skinned, the remainder need only be pressed, one by one, between thumb and forefinger to slip them from the skins ; almonds may be soaked for an hour or so in ice water to whiten them ; discard any yellow or discoloured pistachios, retaining only those that are green. Almonds, in practically any dish, will render it especially agreeable with a Sauternes ; the sweet, tender, incompletely ripened, fresh almonds, skinned, will enhance numberless salads, fish and meat garnishes and desserts. In addition to their sweet flavour, the sharp green accents of coarsely chopped pistachios lend welcome visual relief to any of the puddings or soufflés mentioned above, to mousselines, pâtés, terrines and galantines, etc. Amongst the most exquisite of Sauternes marriages is a blanc-manger (see also " Meats, Poultry and Game " below) ; in the last century it was sweetened almond milk (almonds pounded with

progressive additions of water and twisted in a towel to wring out the " milk ") set with calf's foot jelly ; today, it is a creamy almond milk bavarois (recipes in Escoffier, Montagné and Salles, Bocuse, etc.) – a few bitter almonds pounded with the sweet are essential and it should contain only enough gelatine to hold its form, trembling, when unmoulded. No

The dining-room at Château d'Yquem.

sauce, no décor ; it is a pure thing of great beauty (" Le Taillevent ", Paris, is one of the rare restaurants whose menu lists blanc-manger.)

Almond-pistachio soufflé pudding : in a processor, whirl a fine julienne of candied orange and lemon zests (parboiled, drained, cooked with a spoonful of sugar and a little water until sticky but not caramelized) with about 125 g (4 oz) peeled almonds and half the weight of pistachios, progressively adding 80-100 g (about 3 oz) sugar, then a small glass of Sauternes and, finally, 3 egg yolks ; whisk the whites of the eggs, with a pinch of salt, to soft peaks, fold with the processed mixture, pour into a buttered gratin dish, sprinkle the surface with sugar and cook in a bain-marie in the oven until the surface is completely swelled, with no depression at the centre, and nicely coloured. For a soufflé effect, serve immediately ; warm, it sinks – cold, it settles into a dense, but delicious, pudding.

Seafood and Fish

Oysters : throughout the nineteenth century, Sauternes was considered to be the perfect companion to oysters ; there are those today who find red wine and oysters chic but it is fashionable to shudder at the thought of oysters with Sauternes – well worth trying with a relatively young Sauternes.

Vioulets : the lemony-iodineish-flavoured, yellow insides of vioulets, the leathery, amorphous sea creatures beloved by the Marseillais, strike a stunning match with Sauternes.

Sea urchins : the small violet-quilled Mediterranean sea urchins with intensely coloured, deep-saffron-red corals, in particular, have a unique sweet sea taste that is never better served than by Sauternes. Eaten alive, straight from the shell ; added abundantly to eggs, scrambled to a smooth cream in a bain-marie ; puréed to finish a fish sauce (in which they act as a binder in the same way as egg yolks) ; or incorporated into fish forcemeats and mousselines (see " Pâtés and Terrines " below).

Crustaceans : the sweet firm flesh of crustaceans, in creamy sauces usually heightened by the presence of an eau-de-vie and some wine – Sauternes finds its place here, whatever the originally prescribed wine may have been (*à l'américaine* sauce and its derivatives are best avoided – the tomato base does nothing for Sauternes) ; a gratin of crayfish tails goes perfectly and many a sauce will gain in suavity by the final addition of crayfish butter : instead of the more or less intimidating classical formulas, the carapaces and pincers of crayfish that have been prepared, either *à la nage* or *à la Bordelaise*, can be pounded, passed through a moulinette, shelly debris discarded, the resulting purée whipped into softened butter before being passed through a fine tammy to remove any minute shell fragments – or the purée may be passed alone through the tammy and loosened with a bit of cream before being added to a sauce which is then finished with unflavoured butter.

Squid : the combined sweet savours of squid, freshly picked garden peas and new garden shallots, braised in Sauternes, intermingle wonderfully and find their perfect acccompaniment in no other wine. The " wings " heads and tentacles are chopped, rapidly sautéed with chopped, butter-stewed shallots and combined with parboiled, rinsed and drained rice, chopped tender young leaves of perennial savory, salt and a breath of cayenne, the squid bodies are stuffed with the mixture, tacked with kitchen string at the open end and sautéed in hot olive oil until firmed up ; moistened first with a dash of cognac, then with Sauternes, braised until half-cooked, then smothered with whole, butter-stewed shallots, freshly picked and shelled little peas, a sprinkle of salt ; and finished, tightly closed, over the lowest possible heat for about half an hour, dabs of cream thrown over a few minutes before serving.

Fish : in the choice of fish to accompany Sauternes, the menu-makers of the past made no mistake in relying heavily on turbot, often prepared in a Sauternes court-bouillon – although the choice, in part, may have been dictated by the spectacular possibilities of presentation of a whole turbot, garnished with glistening truffle slices, bouquets of poached oysters and mussels, and trussed crayfish, apparently soaring in for a landing.

Turbot or brill, poached in court-bouillon, are often served with a mousseline sauce (hollandaise lightened with whipped cream) ; a fish velouté, simmered and cleansed for a couple of hours, is a good sauce base for any white fleshed fish – finished with cream, sea urchin purée and butter, it is astounding. Try sturgeon or eel, braised in Sauternes, with a garnish of little glazed onions.

Meats, Poultry and Game

Veal sweetbreads : lambs' sweetbreads are as good, but too small and ragged for an attractive presentation – they serve best fragmented and incorporated into little ragoûts to garnish crusts, bouchées, mousseline-lined darioles, etc. Braise veal sweetbreads in equal parts of Sauternes and demi-glace, reduce the liquid and add cream, reduce again, if necessary, and swirl in a few fragments of butter off the heat, or – utterly basic – arrange the sweetbreads on a bed of mirepoix in an earthenware poêlon, salt lightly, dribble over a small glass of Sauternes, press a sheet of buttered kitchen paper to the surface of the sweetbreads ; cover tightly and sweat over very low heat for about half an hour – a minute or so before serving, discard the paper, grind over pepper, distribute a few dabs of thick cream over the surface and replace the lid. Prepared in this way, the sweetbreads are not really braised but steamed, the buttered paper creating a self-basting effect as the aromatic vapours condense on its surface, continually anointing the sweetbreads as they flow back down. Before cooking, the sweetbreads should be soaked in cold water for several hours, generously covered with cold water in a large saucepan, brought slowly to simmering point and kept below the simmer for about 15 minutes, then refreshed in cold water, surface membranes, fragments of fat and cartilaginous tubes removed ; to retain all of their succulence they should not boil either during the blanching process or while braising, nor should they be pressed under weight.

Chicken, duck, pheasant, partridge or quail, plainly roasted : roast duck or game birds with buttered and grilled apple rings form an ideal garnish-liaison with Sauternes. Duck is sometimes rubbed with honey and coarsely ground pepper before roasting – for this to make sense, it should be a domestic duck, well-done. When three-quarters done, the fat can be removed from the pan and Sauternes dribbled over, then basted repeatedly to form a glaze. A good squeeze of bitter or Seville orange does wonders for roast duck, either rare or well-done, or it can sharpen and refine a duck's braising juices.

Stuffed and braised duck : remove the oil glands, slit the back of the neck skin, remove neck and wing tips and bone the duck (mallard or musk) except for shoulder joint and legs, without piercing or cutting the skin ; from the neck opening, turn it inside out, freeing the carcass with fingertips and small knife tip, snip, leaving tail vertebrae intact and stuff with something rustic : parboiled, squeezed, chopped chard leaves, brousse or other fresh white cheese, herbs, breadcrumb and egg, chopped sautéed giblets and onion, garlic persillade... Truss into its original shape, roast for half an hour to rid it of excess fat and colour it lightly : transfer to an oval cocotte of a size to just contain it, splash over some Sauternes and enough stock to nearly immerse it (made from carcass, neck, wing tips and veal trimmings), and braise for an hour. Remove duck to a shallow oven dish and finish, basting repeatedly with degreased, reduced braising juices until the coat is a glossy caramel ; simmer a handful of blanched olives in the remaining juices and finish with a trickle of bitter orange juice.

In the eighteenth century, a *blanc-manger* was a sweetened, almond-flavoured, jellied purée of boiled chicken, perfumed with cinnamon and orange flower water. Respecting the same principles, it can easily be transformed into a savoury entrée of great delicacy : while still warm, separate the flesh from the skin and bones of a slightly underdone roast chicken, cut up coarsely and reduce to a fine purée in a processor, progressively adding almond milk and stiff, melted jelly (made from chicken, veal, calf's foot and aromatics), add half-whipped cream, taste for seasoning, pour into a decorative mould rubbed with almond oil, chill and unmould just before serving.

Pork and apricots : stuff a boned pork loin with dried apricots that have macerated in Sauternes, tie and three-quarters roast it, pour off the fat, add the leftover macerating liquid to the pan, and baste the roast repeatedly to glaze it during the final 15 or 20 minutes ; equally good hot or cold. Or, soak prunes overnight in Sauternes, transfer to a baking dish and poach, covered, in a cool oven for an hour ; sauté lightly floured, seasoned medallions of pork fillet in butter, remove to platter, strain prune liquid into pan with a squeeze of lemon or bitter orange, reduce, add cream, reduce again, surround medallions with prunes and pour over sauce.

Crépinettes of truffled pigs' trotters : ungarnished, to replace the sausages traditionally served in the Bordelais as an accompaniment to oysters or, served alone, garnished with sautéed sliced apples or grilled apple rings. Braise pigs' trotters in stock and Madeira for 3 1/2 to 4 hours, bone and cube them ; add the chopped trimmings, chopped truffles and some of the reduced braising liquid to basic sausage meat (two parts lean pork to one part fat – the meat can be salted down overnight, rinsed free of salt and dried in towels before passing it through the medium blade of a meat grinder –, seasoned with salt, pepper, puréed garlic, allspice, ground dried herbs [thyme, marjoram, savory, oregano] and cognac) ; sandwich layers of trotter flesh between patties of sausage mixture and press together ; press a truffle slice to the surface, wrap in squares of caul and grill until nicely coloured on each side and slightly shrunken.

Braised tongue in a sweet and sour sauce or braised tongue sausage : tongue, parboiled, peeled, split, pierced abundantly with spikes of truffle and lardons rolled in spiced and herbed salt, forced into a large ox gut, tied, pierced here and there with a trussing needle and salted down for a day or two with a mixture of coarse sea salt, dried herbs and spices ; rinsed and dried and braised gently with calves' feet in stock and Sauternes for 5 to 6 hours, braising juices cleansed and reduced, calves' feet boned, cut up and rewarmed in braising juices to garnish the sliced sausage.

Pâtés and Terrines

Foie gras is famous ; many other pâtés or terrines, some counting foie gras in their composition, others not, in particular those based on duck, game or fish, are splendid with Sauternes. Cold pâtés – terrine assemblages enclosed and baked in pastry, usually with aspic jelly poured in after they have cooled – afford elegant presentations but most diners may be observed to remove the pastry and push it aside. The preparation of terrines is much less time-consuming and, in the case of meat terrines, sealed beneath a protective sheet of impermeable fat, their aptitude for improvement over a period of a few days or a couple of weeks as their flavours meld, ripen and deepen, gives them a distinct advantage over pâtés, whose pastry would go sodden and whose jelly would go off with the same treatment.

Meat terrines : the same seasoned sausage mixture as that used for the crépinettes, supplemented by puréed poultry or rabbit livers and veal, eggs, semi-fresh breadcrumbs and chopped, butter-stewed onions or shallots, can serve as a base for any meat terrine.

In addition, there may be included the tender fillets of the meat from which the terrine takes its name – duck, game birds, rabbit, hare –, cubed or cut into long strips and marinated, usually in fortified wines or eau-de-vie or both, with truffles, herbs, etc. The hare's blood, as well as its puréed liver must go into a hare terrine and, in a woodcock terrine, the puréed innards, excepting the gizzard, are worked into the forcemeat ; the remainder of the animal's flesh, finely ground or puréed, pork back fat and raw ham, diced or cut into strips, truffles, chopped, diced or cut into thick sticks ; chopped pistachios are always welcome, foie gras is often added, either in pieces or worked into the forcemeat to heighten the silken texture (or foie gras may be the principal element, whole lobes of raw, truffled, marinated foie gras embedded in the basic forcemeat), and sometimes sweetbreads (for a sweetbread terrine, embed whole, partially braised sweetbreads in the forcemeat, into which their reduced braising juices have been incorporated).

When the various elements have been cubed or diced, everything, including marinades, is mixed together and will improve – the surface packed smooth, a splash of white wine poured over and tightly covered – if refrigerated overnight, as the truffle penetrates and all the flavours intermingle, before being packed into bard-lined terrines ; when cut into sticks and strips, they are held in their marinade until the terrines are assembled, with alternating layers of forcemeat and mosaic patterns of flesh, truffle and fat strung the length of the terrine.

One or two bay leaves are pressed to the surface and they are cooked, covered, in a bain-marie in a moderate oven ; an hour or slightly more will do for smaller terrines, an hour and a half or more for larger – when done, the abundant cooking juices will be clear and a trussing needle plunged into the centre should come out warm at the tip. They are cooled under weight, a board or a piece of heavy cardboard cut to the inside dimensions of the terrine, protected from contact with juices by a sheet of foil, and a tin of canned goods or other object placed on top ; to keep, melted lard is poured over when cool and they are refrigerated, covered.

Subtle interplays of flavour and beautiful cross-sectional patterns can be created by dividing the basic forcemeat, finishing one half with hare, the other with white meats ;

" *Summers from a distant past are aflame in bottles of Yquem.* "
François Mauriac – Le Baiser au lépreux.

140

marinating the hare fillets, ham strips and half the truffles and lardons in one marinade ; the white meats and remaining truffles and lardons in another (Madeira or Port for the first, Sauternes for the second, for instance) ; and alternating dark mosaic garnish between two thin beds of light forcemeat with light garnish between two beds of dark. With the carcasses, a calf's foot and veal stock, a wonderful jelly can be made (when nearly cool but before beginning to jell, it may be flavoured with Sauternes) to accompany these terrines, chopped.

For a creamy liver terrine, simmer a large handful of semi-fresh breadcrumbs with rich stock until reduced to a paste and mix with a pounded garlic clove. In a processor, add to this panade the marrow dug from a beef leg bone, a pound of chicken livers, salt, pepper, cayenne, mixed herbs, whiz to a purée, pass through a fine sieve and whisk in 3 eggs, 10 cl (3 or 4 fl oz) cream and a dash of eau-de-vie ; pour into a buttered terrine, cook in a bain-marie in the oven for an hour, or until the centre is firm. When nearly cooled, unmould, press plastic wrap to the surface to protect it from air, refrigerate and serve the following day.

A fish terrine for Sauternes : a buttered, narrow rectangular terrine, sides and bottom lined crosswise with overlapping sole fillets, slashed membrane surfaces facing in (ends unlined), filled with sea urchin mousseline flecked with chopped pistachios, the extremities of the fillets folded over the surface to form a roulade, buttered kitchen paper pressed to the surface, poached in bain-marie, unmoulded when tepid (first turn the terrine upside-down with a cake grill held to its surface to drain off any loose liquid), chilled (protected by plastic wrap) and coated with fish jelly.

Monkfish is a good choice for the mousseline, or whiting will do – it is only a vehicle for the sea urchin flavour. The corals (10–12 cl/3–4 fl oz) are puréed with 250 g (1/2 lb) trimmed fillets before incorporating an egg white and seasoning and passing the mixture through a fine nylon tammy ; pack in metal bowl, press plastic film to the surface, and hold on ice for at least an hour before beginning to mount progressively with cream (25–30 cl/8–10 fl oz), a few spoons at at time, every quarter of an hour or so.

A fumet, made from the carcasses of the sole and whatever fish served for the mousseline, is the jelly base. Unlike meat jellies which, if carefully prepared, need no clarification – and are the better for it – fish fumets are never absolutely limpid ; they are clarified with egg white and, unless made from turbot carcasses, need the added support of commercial gelatine. The jelly may, obviously, be flavoured with Sauternes.

Salads

The marriage of Sauternes with vinaigrettes and other preparations in which vinegar plays a role can be quite surprisingly successful (this theme is one of Pierre Meslier's passions and he insists on the importance of a strong dose of vinegar) ; wild rabbit, for instance, roasted and incorporated, sliced or cut up while still warm, into a vinaigrette salad – any juices which escape should be added to the vinaigrette.

Salade Francillon : a classic of sorts which began its career as a literary conversational fantasy in Alexandre Dumas fils's play, *Francillon* (in which it was named " Salade Japonaise "). It is a vinaigrette salad of potatoes, mussels and truffles, seasoned with Sauternes (" ... Château-Yquem si possible ", says the play's protagonist). It immediately became fashionable and eventually was canonized amongst the classics in Escoffier's *Le Guide culinaire*, where the presentation was much more rational but the Sauternes had mysteriously been replaced by Chablis. Prepared with Sauternes, it is lovely and perfectly accompanied by the same or a different Sauternes: firm-fleshed kidney potatoes boiled in their skins, peeled while hot and sliced into a bowl containing Sauternes; mussels steamed open with chopped celery and onion, a crushed garlic clove, thyme, bay and a splash of Sauternes, and then shelled; truffles sliced and warmed (without ever simmering), covered, in a trickle each of olive oil and Sauternes, salt and pepper; potatoes drained and tossed cautiously with the other two ingredients in a vinaigrette containing nothing but salt, a generous grinding of pepper, the best red wine vinegar and olive oil available, and an additional splash of Sauternes; salad bowl covered and left at room temperature for an hour before serving; chopped chives and freshly plucked, flat-leafed parsley may be scattered over (the wine drained from the potatoes can be added to the strained mussel liquid for use in a sauce or a soup).

Lemon and cream are combined in the same way as vinegar and oil to dress salads: chicken breast (raw, cut into strips and sautéed for a minute); fish and shellfish (poached in fumet or a mixture of fumet and Sauternes, the juices reduced to a syrup and added to the sauce – examples are: sole fillets cut into strips or sliced scallops, warmed *to below simmering point* and held, covered, off the heat, for a minute or until no longer translucent; prawns, peeled while raw, a fumet made of their shells, in which they are poached only until firm); the shelled tails of crayfish, first prepared *à la nage*, the same purée as that used for the crayfish butter stirred into the sauce; brains (poached in vinegar court-bouillon, cooled and sliced, sieved brain trimmings and mustard incorporated into the sauce). Raw mushrooms, thinly sliced and tossed in a bit of lemon juice, can be stirred into the sauce before it is added to any of the above; sliced almonds or peeled and halved green almonds, chopped pistachios, pine nuts, etc., can also be added.

Fig and ham salad: crush fresh mint leaves in the lemon juice and leave to macerate for 10 minutes or so before straining, seasoning and stirring in the cream; peel and cut a cross half-way down each fig, partially open it out by pressing from the sides, arrange on serving dish, sprinkle with a fine julienne cut from thin slices of prosciutto (*jambon cru*) from which all fat has been removed, spoon over the sauce, scatter over a few threads of ham and decorate with mint leaves. Enemies of mint can substitute the tender shoots and leaves of wild fennel.

SUGGESTIONS FROM MAÎTRES CUISINIERS AND YQUEM ENTHUSIASTS

The preceding ideas are meant to be no more than suggestions. Above all, they are not to be taken as a set of rigid rules but merely as a selection of possibilities with which to play around. One's own palate must be the ultimate judge.

For those who feel that this text is tainted by irrational prejudice, let it be said that some Yquem enthusiasts find that, with very old vintages in which faint memories of chocolate are present in the bouquet and on the palate, a discreetly sweetened, bitter chocolate dessert goes well; many have suggested fresh red fruits such as raspberries or strawberries, and two professionals – Henri van Ranst, director of the

143

restaurant, Villa Lorraine in Brussels, and Jean Bardet, proprietor-chef of the restaurant that bears his name in Châteauroux – have recommended pistachio ice-cream with Château d'Yquem.

Foie gras and Yquem, on the other hand, form a classic marriage accepted by everyone. For those who would like to prepare their own foie gras, the recipe of Paul Haeberlin (L'Auberge de l'Ill, Illhausern) is simple, classic and perfect : the whole liver is seasoned with salt and spices, macerated overnight with a sprinkling of cognac and port, pressed into a terrine with pieces of truffle embedded in it, cooked, covered, in a bain-marie, in a gentle oven (150° C/300° F) for 40 minutes, cooled in the bain-marie and melted goose fat poured over to seal it ; it will improve with a bit of maturing and may be kept, refrigerated, for a couple of weeks.

Amongst hot foie gras preparations that work wonders with Sauternes, Frédy Girardet's "foie gras de canard à la vinaigrette" (Girardet, Crissier, Switzerland), the slices of liver rapidly sautéed and sauced with a warm walnut oil vinaigrette made with chopped shallots cooked in vinegar, requires only a few minutes from kitchen to table ; Paul Bocuse (Paul Bocuse, Collonges-au-Mont-d'Or) recommends a "petit pâté chaud de ris de veau et foie gras" (sweetbreads and foie gras baked in pastry).

Other suggestions are : fresh foie gras in truffle sauce (Périgueux) and fresh fettucine with white truffles (Dr Overton, Fort Worth, Texas) ; roast saddle of hare with a light, spicy sauce (Frédy Girardet) ; fresh truffles steamed in Sauternes, the reduced Sauternes mounted with butter (Pierre Troisgros, Roanne) ; soufflé au fromage (Prince de Metternich). Monsieur Nathaniel Johnston, of the venerable firm of Bordeaux wine merchants of the same name, writes of his astonished delight at the perfect marriage of roast pheasants and a 1934 Yquem.

Professor Paul Paris (Washington University, Saint Louis, Missouri) matches different ages and styles of Yquem with different kinds of food : as examples, he suggests 1967 with lobster and butter sauce, 1962 with salmon in cream sauce, 1961 with oysters or other raw shellfish, 1959 with duck in a light orange or honey sauce, and 1945 with cake, cream and strawberries. Mr Rodenstock (Germany) figures that different kinds of food impose different serving temperatures ; he suggests 6°–8° C (43°–46° F) with foie gras, 8°–10° C (46°–50° F) with desserts and 10°–12° C (50°–53° F) with roquefort or stilton.

Nico Ladenis (Restaurant Chez-Nico, Shinfield and London) explains that he uses a bit of Sauternes in all of his fish sauces to lend them complexity, adding it only when finishing the sauce so that the wine will not be altered by cooking. Jean-Paul Bonin, chef of the Crillon kitchens, Paris, mentions the following preparations in which he uses Sauternes : cassolette d'huitres aux choux ; barbue en portefeuille aux poireaux ; médaillon de veau au raifort et blettes ; mousse de chèvre au vin d'Yquem. Nico Ladenis serves pears, cooked in red wine, finely sliced, coated with Sauternes sabayon, sprinkled with icing sugar and glazed beneath high heat ; Georges Blanc (Chez La Mère Blanc, Vonnas) does the same with sliced white peaches, scattering over wild strawberries at the moment of service. With Sauternes, Georges Blanc also recommends his "panaché de la mer au Sauternes et au curry", scallops and a selection of fish fillets cut into pieces of a regular size, sprinkled with a few drops of water to create steam and cooked very rapidly in a hot oven, sauced with a shallot- and garlic-flavoured reduction of Sauternes and cream, finished with a pinch of curry, a squeeze of lemon and a ladle of emulsified butter.

André Guillot, retired *maître-cuisinier*, idol of many of France's younger chefs, has created in honour of Ghislaine Bavoillot, " le homard Ghislaine au Château d'Yquem ", lobsters parboiled in salt water with seaweed, cooled in their water, shelled and sweated in butter, then simmered gently in a reduction of the cooking juices, Yquem and cream, removed and kept warm while the sauce is finished with a sieved mixture of the lobster innards and legs, a few raisins, butter and thick cream, salt, pepper and paprika. Roger Vergé (Moulin de Mougins, Mougins) recommends a " fricassée de homard à la crème de Sauternes ", boiled, shelled lobster rewarmed in a sauce drawn from the crushed and broken shells and legs flamed in cognac, a lightly tomatoed mirepoix, Sauternes, cream and a sprig of tarragon.

Claude Peyrot (Le Vivarois, Paris) prepares a " fricassée de homard au Yquem et carottes nouvelles " and suggests " jeunes poireaux nouveaux en crème d'Yquem " (tender young leeks with Yquem and cream). Michel Guérard (Les Prés d'Eugénie, Eugénie-les-Bains) uses Yquem in the preparation of his " aile de poulette lardée de foie gras aux herbes potagères " (chicken breast " larded " with foie gras prepared with garden herbs) and recommends, to accompany Yquem, " raviole de truffes à la crème de mousserons et de morilles " (truffle ravioli with a cream of wild mushrooms) or, simply, roast duckling with freshly picked little garden peas.

Bérengère de Lur Saluces.

Yannick Cam (Le Pavillon, Washington, DC) prepares an Yquem jelly in which is poached an exotic, white-fleshed fruit from South America, cherimoya, the flavour of which has memories of strawberry, raspberry and pear, with a touch of cinnamon; he also suggests scallops in Sauternes and cream, flavoured with fresh ginger, a feuilletée of foie gras and truffles with a reduction of Yquem and *jus blond* and a " Bavarois d'amandes " (blanc-manger in a mould lined with lady-fingers) accompanied by an Yquem-flavoured crème anglaise.

With a glass of Yquem, the marquis Bertrand de Lur Saluces professed a particular affection for the pastry from south-west France, called *pastis*. André Daguin's pastis gascon (l'Hôtel de France, Auch) consists of a pastry dough made of flour, water, egg and goose fat, stretched paper-thin in the same way as a strudel or phyllo dough, cut into rounds which are stacked, alternately garnished, first with a sprinkling of sugar, armagnac, orange flower water and goose fat, then with finely sliced apples macerated in armagnac, and so forth, baked and served hot, tepid or cold. A Béarnaise pastry which also takes the name of *pastis* is a rustic cousin to the brioche, flavoured with eau-de-vie. Either is obviously a good accompaniment to Sauternes.

First prize for the most sybaritic " favourite souvenir of Yquem and the table " goes to Paul Bocuse for his memory of a dish savoured in Hong Kong, chicken and pineapple cooked in Château d'Yquem, 1928, accompanied by a bottle of the same.

COLLECTORS, TASTINGS AND VINTAGES

An infectious wind has recently swept the globe, a sort of *folie des grandeurs* which consists in the organization of what are familiarly known as " vertical tastings " of as many vintages as possible of the greatest and rarest wines in the world and which, no doubt, elicits a certain competitive spirit amongst collectors and nations.

Celebrational rumblings in anticipation of the bicentenary presence of the Lur Saluces family at Yquem began in the spring of 1983 in Los Angeles with a two-day marathon tasting of sixty-six vintages of Château d'Yquem ranging from 1978 to 1858, organized by a group of American collectors – Geoffrey Troy, Bipin Desai, Edward Lazarus and Dr Bradford Klein – with the participation of M. Tawfiq Khoury and Dr Ben Ichinose, possessors of prodigious cellars.

Not to be outdone by the Americans, a group of collectors, professionals and journalists organized, in Brussels in the autumn of 1984, a tasting of sixty-seven vintages from 1980 to 1867, also stretched over two days (these two records, however, must be considered a tie, for the Brussels tasting included a pirate vintage, 1930, in which no Yquem was made). In March 1985, in Australia, M. Greg Scott organized a tasting of fifty Yquems from this century to which comte Alexandre de Lur Saluces brought the fifty-first, an 1899. Others, more modest in extent but no less awe-inspiring as to the quality of the vintages, have been recently organized in Germany and at Château d'Yquem.

The notes of the American tasting were published, unsigned, in *The Underground Wine-letter*, a publication on which all of the organizers are collaborators, and those from Brussels in *Gault-Millau Magazine*, both employing the standard formula of rating by

The Brussels tasting, 1984.
Vintages tasted during the second day
(following pages).

147

attributing to each wine a figure in relation to 20, the theoretical figure of ultimate perfection (the American notes rated the 1861 20/20). The notes, presented by Jo Gryn, for the Brussels tasting represent the average of all twelve tasters' notes. Therefore, although seven out of twelve rated the 1945 20/20, its average rating was 19.6 (1947 received five 20s, 1921 five 20s, 1955 three 20s, 1929 three 20s, 1868 three 20s and 1953 two 20s).

More instructive than the notes of either individual tasting is the fact that those given at the two tastings for the most celebrated vintages of this century (1976, 1975, 1971, 1970, 1967, 1955, 1953, 1949, 1947, 1945, 1937, 1934, 1929, 1928, 1921, 1900) correspond very closely. And that, for the first time in a forty-year career, such a seasoned taster as Robert Goffard, one of the great " noses " on the European vinicultural scene and one who believes, in principle, that the magical figure of ultimate perfection is never attained in an imperfect world, gave 20/20 notes to four vintages : 1953, 1947, 1945 and 1921 (and 19/ 20 to 1971, 1962, 1929 and 1900) !

So much for the greatest of the great. Upon reading the 133 notes from these two tastings, it is most saddening to find so many lovely wines, each exquisite in a minor key, pigeon-holed and labelled with an anonymous and mediocre figure. One wonders how, under other circumstances, far from the crushing proximity of the giants, tasted alone or placed with respect on a menu with a dish conceived to etch in relief its special qualities, one of these wines might fare with the specialists. Recently at a dinner given at Yquem, following a tasting of fifteen vintages from 1976 to 1928 (no world record, but an exhausting exercise whose pleasure is purely analytical and intellectual), a 1944 was served on the roquefort (which, despite its reputation as a perfect partner to Yquem, can at times diminish one's perception of the complexity of certain vintages). The vintage claims no reputation and the wine, tasted alone, seemed to have slightly rough edges, an untypical violence ; when drunk with the cheese, it burst into song – for a moment, it was the most beautiful wine in the world, outshining all of the proud and famous vintages that had so studiously been noted and rated throughout the afternoon. This big, rather rough but beautiful, forty-year-old was unusual but many vintages, judged to be " minor ", have produced long-lived wines that often retain a freshness and a delicacy denied to the huge super-vintages ; their published tasting notes are rarely commensurate with the degree of pleasure that they can bring to the table. Moreover, the marathon tastings of old wines, quite apart from the varying sensibilities of the tasters and the inevitable decline of sensory perception as the palate becomes increasingly fatigued, can only lead to a judgement of individual bottles which may or may not, depending upon how they have been cared for over the years, be genuinely representative of their vintages ; it is rare that a venerable bottle of a prestigious vintage is so privileged as to have remained, undisturbed, in a perfect cellar from the time of its bottling to that of its uncorking.

In the context of this book, where the purpose of vintage notes is to give the reader a general idea of the qualities of a given vintage at the present time, it would be unfair, both to the wine and to the reader, to give precisely rated notes. The following notes, an amalgam assembled from records kept at Yquem, answers to queries, books and other recent publications, are deliberately selective as to the older vintages ; an omission, however, does not necessarily imply a negative judgement. In addition to those listed from the nineteenth century, Mr Hardy Rodenstock (who has recently celebrated tasting his 100th vintage of Yquem, an 1881, who, in 1983 in *Alles Uber Wein*, published tasting notes for ninety-five Yquem vintages and who is also preparing a book on Yquem) gives high notes to the following: 1854, 1855, 1863, 1876, 1878 and 1879.

The notes have been selected for clarity. Technical vocabulary has been avoided whenever possible. Quotations are followed, in parentheses, by the source and the year of tasting. The notes from the Institut d'Œnologie de Bordeaux are remarkable for their severity and those from Yquem for their discretion. Certain pairs of consecutive vintages of fabulous reputation, usually nineteenth-century, are commonly called twin vintages, which explains their being presented in this way.

Gras (fat) should be understood to mean " full, round, supple, ripe ... " (a " fat " Yquem will present heavy, lazy " tears " or legs). *Rôti* (roast) has sometimes been translated as " full-flavoured "; the word should be accepted in the double sense of referring to the specific flavour of *grains rôtis*, the grapes withered by noble rot, and also to associations with roast or grilled meats or bread, often with charred or smoky suggestions.

The preoccupation with *acescence*, or volatile acidity, in certain notes is explained by the fact that all wines made from grapes that have been altered by botrytis have naturally a higher level of volatile acidity than wines made from normally ripened grapes (unless there has been an accident in vinification); the level of imperceptibility is also higher. The volatile acidity in a Sauternes is said to be *levurienne*, or yeastian, in origin rather than *bactérienne*, which is to say that, although the acid is volatile, it is not acetic acid (vinegar). A note that indicates " no volatile acidity " means that its presence is imperceptible. In fact, without (imperceptible) volatile acid, there would be no bouquet.

Vintage Notes

1753 : Recorded in the Yquem cellar book on 5 June 1821, is the sale of fifty half-bottles of the vintage, 1753, to M. Guestier, a merchant who was unlikely to buy a sixty-eight-year-old wine, especially in half-bottles, if it was in less than perfect condition.

1784 : Discovered in an undivulged quarter of Paris by Mr Rodenstock, this is presumed to be one of the 250 bottles of 1784 purchased by Thomas Jefferson from comte Louis-Amédée de Lur Saluces in 1788. Engraved in the glass are the words, " L. Sauvage d'Yquem ", and the letters, " T.J. " Tasted at Weisbaden on 14 October 1985, Michael Broadbent, in a Christie's catalogue, reports that " the wine was perfect in every sense : colour, bouquet and taste ".

1787 : From the same source as above. Engraved in the glass are the words, " Château d'Yquem ", and the letters, " TH. J. ".

One of the two bottles unearthed by Mr Rodenstock was tasted at Yquem on 4 May 1985. The following excerpt from a letter tells the story : " Mr Rodenstock had taken the care to cover the original sealing wax with a new layer of wax which we proceeded to break, then the cork was removed with the greatest of precautions for, in all probability, it was the original cork. This suite of events sufficed in itself to fill me with joy ; but the astonishing thing is that the wine was excellent ... not only liquorous and still alcoholic, but very harmonious. I was stupefied to discover something so vibrant and so alive, so characteristic of a great Yquem vintage. " (Comte A. de Lur Saluces, 1985).

1847 : The vintage made famous by the grand duke Constantine of Russia for whom a record price 900-litre tun was bottled in gold-engraved crystal decanters. No notes. Alexandre de Lur Saluces owns one bottle, offered to him by one of the great Yquem collectors, Dr Nils Stormby, Swedish cancer specialist. Picking began 25 September.

1848 : Mr Rodenstock, in his notes, describes this wine at the time of opening as faded with memories of greatness. Twenty-four hours later, " The wine now presented a long finish and a delicious 'liqueur'. " The second day's tasting is awarded the ultimate score of perfection (tasted in 1983). Picking began 26 September.

1858 : " Absolutely sensational ... majestic wine which still has a great future. " (Rodenstock, 1980). Picking began 25 September.

1861 : " Totally incredible wine. One of the great wine experiences of a lifetime ... a nectar that should see the next century in fine shape. Dark brown colour, amber gold tones. Rich, intriguing nose. Rich, deep, liqueur-like texture ... Very long finish. Perfect balance. Exquisite. " (*The Underground Wineletter*, 1983). Twice tasted by A. de Lur Saluces who was both times astounded by its vitality, depth and complexity. Picking began 24 September.

1864-1865 : Famous " twin " vintages, still likely to be in prime condition if well cellared (both receive very high notes from Mr Rodenstock). Picking began 26 September in 1864 ; 15 September in 1865.

1867 : " Very deep old amber ... amazingly rich bouquet – deep caramelly but clean ... rich, meaty flavour, lovely acidity, firm and surprisingly sound. " (Michael Broadbent, *The Great Vintage Wine Book*, four tastings, 1970-1972). Picking began 28 September.

1868 : " Beautiful brown with orange reflections. Fantastic freshness ; everything is harmonious, a spirituous, rose-scented unctuousness, reduced fruits mingled with toasted scents, with caramel, café, plum ... A fabulous miracle. " (Jo Gryn, *Gault-Millau*, 1984). Picking began 4 October.

1869 : Great vintage, often compared with 1921. " Rich, maderized nose, slightly burnt. Very concentrated. Raisined. Rich. Caramelized, sweet, vanilla flavour. Touch of spice. Long finish. Delicious. " (*The Underground Wineletter*, 1983). Picking began 24 September.

1870 : " Majestic wine, marvellous scent of honey ... very rich finish. " (Rodenstock, 1983). Picking began 20 September.

1871 : " ... nose of caramel, vanilla and chocolate. Very nice flavour. Nutty, caramel quality with some vanilla. Elegant. Round. Sweet. Nice finish. Touch of acid on the finish. " (*The Underground Wineletter*, 1983). Picking began 29 September.

1874-1875 : Celebrated twins. High notes from Mr Rodenstock for the 1874 (1977) ; no notes for 1875. Picking began 25 September in 1874 ; 26 September in 1875.

1883 : " I have been privileged to taste and drink many vintages of Yquem. The most extraordinary and surprising was the 1883. " (Michael Broadbent, 1984). Picking began 6 October.

1890 : " Bronze amber colour. Fine old honeyed bouquet. Dryish, strong flavoured, spirity. Lovely dry honeyed finish. " (Jeffrey Benson and Alastair Mackenzie, *Sauternes*, 1975). Picking began 6 October.

1892 : " Bouquet leaves one wordless : incredibly sound, classic, lovely ... medium sweetness and body. A very positive, good, crisp flavour ... Dry finish ... " (Michael Broadbent, *Decanter*, 1984). Picking began 17 September.

1893 : Vintage of mythical reputation. " Firm colour. Nose reminiscent of port, of old muscat, of fruit, of currants, of caramel ... unctuous, long finish with marked but not excessive sweetness. Remarkable form without the slightest fault in this perfect wine ... " (Jo Gryn, *Gault-Millau*, 1984). Unheard-of weather. Heat set in the first of March, hot, dry summer. Picking began 28 August.

1896 : " Very good wine. Very complex bouquet of crystallized fruits. " (Yquem, 1982) ; " Excellent classic nose ... Sweet, fairly full-bodied, rich, excellent flavour, balance and acidity. A very fine positive wine. " (Michael Broadbent, *Decanter*, 1984). Picking began 21 September.

1899-1900 : More famous twins.

1899 : " Warm amber. Pale for an old Yquem. Bouquet ... lightly scented, fragrant ferns ... after half an hour ... toasted cream, perfection. Still fairly sweet but with the charm and lovely delicacy of a Lafite 1899. Gentle but crisp crème brûlée flavour. " (Michael Broadbent, *Decanter*, 1894).

1900 : " Deep amber. Rich, concentrated bouquet, melting, burnt fruit, plums, crystallized fruit, almond and marmalade. Graceful evolution on the palate with great harmony. Mellow with a remarkable caramel and burnt sugar finish. A very great wine ... " (Jo Gryn, *Gault-Millau*, 1984). Picking began 19 September both years.

1904 : " Amber colour, lots of fruit and body, long sweet finish. Magnificent wine. " (Rodenstock, 1977). Picking began 17 September.

1908 : " Deep gold, superb rich honeyed nose, full of fruit, delicious wine, long rich finish. " (Jeffrey Benson and Alastair Mackenzie, *Sauternes*, 1975). Picking began 16 September.

1909 : " Deep, rich, warm amber with very green rim ... Overall effect rich and thick. On the palate still fairly sweet, full bodied, very rich, with remarkable length and acidity. Flavour of marron glacé. " (Michael Broadbent, *Decanter*, 1984). Picking began 21 September.

1913 : Wartime bottling – dark green half-bottles. Light-bodied, floral, astonishingly fresh and young (1982). Picking began 18 September.

1914 : " Deep gold ... Rich, pretty nose of muscat, *rôti*, orange. Long, elegant, honeyed palate supported by a touch of iodine. Finishes a bit short but as fat and mellow as one could wish. " (Jo Gryn, *Gault-Millau*, 1984). Picking began 23 September.

1916 : " Deep Gold. Fine rich honeyed nose, some signs of age. Still holding with fruit in centre, drying finish. " (Jeffrey Benson and Alastair Mackenzie, *Sauternes*, 1974). Picking began 26 September.

1917 : " Deep gold, nose a bit severe, but finishes full and round. " (Rodenstock, 1981). Picking began 19 September.

1918 : "Golden yellow colour. Unusual nose, minty and slightly herbal with vanilla undertones. Light and relatively dry with just a touch of sweetness. Nutty quality. Touch of bitterness ..." (*The Underground Wineletter*, 1983). Picking began 24 September.

1919 : "Surprising, pretty yellow-gold colour. Delicate nose recalling iodine and walnuts. Slightly oxidized but well preserved, with a mellow, mouthfilling finish." (Jo Gryn, *Gault-Millau*, 1984). Picking began 24 September.

1920 : Fine wine that has too often suffered from an unfair comparison with the 1921. "Deep gold, superb full nose, slight signs of age." (Jeffrey Benson and Alastair Mackenzie, *Sauternes*, 1977). Picking began 15 September.

1921 : Often characterized as the greatest white wine vintage of the century. "Suave, seductive, exotic liqueur-like aroma of candied fruits with floral touches, a scent of peppery yellow roses. Sumptuous, enveloping warmth. Ripe, complex palate. Rich in savours with spicy overtones and mouth vapours recalling green chartreuse, the ensemble contained by a remarkable overall homogeneity conferring upon the wine an aura of timelessness." (Robert Goffard, 1984). Picking began 13 September.

1922 : "Deep gold. Full rich deep nose, slight signs of age. Good rich fruit, slightly dry finish." (Jeffrey Benson and Alastair Mackenzie, *Sauternes*, 1976). Picking began 12 September.

1923 : "Lovely gold. Discreet, delicate nose recalling green leafy things. Good balance and harmony but lacks corpulence." (Jo Gryn, *Gault-Millau*, 1984). Picking began 1 October.

1924 : Fragile, ethereal, suave, complex ... Published notes on this vintage are disparate. "Very promising, deep gold colour, very fruity and liquorous with marvellous finish." (Rodenstock, 1982). Picking began 26 September.

1926 : "Lovely warm amber ; low keyed, classic crème brûlée Sémillon, honeyed and peppery ; medium sweet, good body, balance and acidity. Slightly stern and lacking fragrance, but fine and with quality endorsed by the aftertaste." (Michael Broadbent, *Decanter*, 1984). Picking began 28 September.

1928 : A summit of subtlety, quiet elegance and balance with a great future. "Very great wine, intense bouquet. Good balance, lots of character. Very long finish." (Yquem, 1982). Picking began 24 September.

1929 : An extraordinarily rich wine, bigger than life ; mahogany-coloured. By Yquem's standards, less perfectly balanced than its twin of the preceding year, none the less a great, long-lived and much admired vintage. "Very deep colour. Very aromatic and complex bouquet. Scent of crystallized fruit. Very rich, very fat and very full. A bit too sweet but a remarkable wine in spite of a slightly hot finish." (l'Institut d'Œnologie de Bordeaux, 1978). Despite ending on a typically negative note, this represents very high praise, coming from the IOB. Picking began 20 September.

1933 : "Clear yellow gold, floral nose of lime blossom and of broom. Light structure supported by freshness." (Jo Gryn, *Gault-Millau*, 1984). Picking began 18 September.

1934 : A wine with soft edges, melting flavours, nice balance, more elegance than power. "Clear brilliant yellow with a nose recalling muscat, mint, tobacco, marron glacé. Well balanced, good persistence, suave, pleasant and spicy palate." (Jo Gryn, *Gault-Millau*, 1984). Picking began 7 September.

1936 : "Amber colour, golden to the rim. Dusty nose, some vanilla underneath. Some sweetness. Light with a touch of spice and a hint of earth in the flavour. Unusual but attractive. Nice balance and finish." (*The Underground Wineletter*, 1983). Picking began 21 September.

1937 : Astonishing wine, aglow with luminous, sparkling amber, shot with orange flame. Intricate, vibrant nose and palate with a bell-like clarity (1985). Published notes are generally dithyrambic. Amongst the scents and savours mentioned by different tasters are oak, caramel, honey, apricot, vanilla and armagnac. Picking began 21 September.

1939 : "Amber colour, golden to the rim. Caramel nose. Slightly burnt with a hint of spice. Still some sweetness. Light but rounded. Trace of cedary spiciness. Some acid on the finish. Quite lovely." (*The Underground Wineletter*, 1983). Picking began 25 September.

1940 : "Deep gold. Superb rich nose, slight signs of age. Good fruit on extract, good finish, slightly drying." (Jeffrey Benson and Alastair Mackenzie, *Sauternes*, 1977). More recently, good notes from the Los Angeles tasting (1983) and poor notes from the Brussels tasting (1984). Picking began 30 September.

1942 : Dusky amber robe with a touch of burnt siena. Sombre, restrained, subtle ... gentle and complex, understated, unveils itself unhurriedly. " ... green rimmed ... low keyed, gentle, fragrant, medium sweet, full bodied ... Broad style. Good dry acid finish." (Michael Broadbent, *Decanter*, 1984); "Fabulous bouquet of fruits and flowers. Very long finish. A suave wine with an after taste of candied orange peel."

(*La Revue du vin de France*, 1975). Picking began 5 October.

1943 : "Very bright, warm amber ; very good classic Sauternes nose, lively and forthcoming. Alcoholic, peppery. After three hours, chocolaty. Medium sweet, fairly full-bodied yet some softness. Rich, positive, fragrant, high alcohol and good acid balance. Aftertaste like the crisp caramel crust on crème brûlée. Touch of volatile acidity on nose and end taste." (Michael Broadbent, *Decanter*, 1984). Picking began 14 September.

1944 : Limpid caramel ; rough-hewn Yquem, a bit awkward when first poured, rapidly pulled itself together, wonderful with roquefort (1985). Good notes from the Los Angeles tasting (1983) and poor notes from the Brussels tasting (1984). Picking began 19 September.

1945 : A huge wine. "Register of rich scents : Russia leather, amber, dried currants. Rigid, vertical maturity with a certain austerity. Restrained, honeyed mellowness with still a taste of oak. Highly personal balance with great allure and an assured future." (Robert Goffard, 1984). Picking began 10 September.

1946 : "Straw yellow. Light, spicy nose. The mouth is fresh. Well made, melting, fat, elegant and clean." (Jo Gryn, *Gault-Millau*, 1984). Picking began 9 October.

1947 : Sumptuous wine from one of the hottest and driest summers of the century, similar climatic conditions to those of 1929. "Very good vintage. Very agreeable today. Slightly *maderized* [oxidized]. Ageing potential : 50 years." (Yquem, 1982); "Delicious floral odour in which are mingled locust flowers and lime blossom, narcissus and, at the same time, a sweet scent with a note of crystallized orange which will be repeated in the richness of the palate. Exceptional intensity of sugars, perfectly integrated and thrown into relief by a lovely freshness recalling the aromatic notes. The softened contours of a firm alcoholic structure ensure a perfect balance." (Robert Goffard, 1984). Picking began 13 September.

1948 : Classic, solidly constituted Yquem that, from its inception, has been obscured by the spectacular reputations of 1945, 1947 and 1949. Vigorous, elegant, well-balanced wine. Received very high notes at tasting at Château d'Yquem (1985), good notes elsewhere. Picking began 24 September.

1949 : "Deep gold. Deep complex nose with enormous depth of quality. Full, tight, luscious, huge, closed, long way to go." (Jeffrey Benson and Alastair Mackenzie, *Sauternes*, 1978) ; "Round, elegant and delicious with a long finish. Outstanding wine." (*The Underground Wineletter*, 1983) ; "... colossal depth, tremendous fruit and finesse, magnificent balance." (Rodenstock, 1983). Picking began 26 September.

1950 : Severe but luscious Yquem with a distinct note of bitter almond in the background which distresses some people and ravishes others ; splendid with a blanc-manger (1982). Picking began 20 September.

1951 : No Yquem.

1952 : No Yquem.

1953 : Delicate lacy wine, lean and elegant, more breeding than volupté. Great style. "Rather special nose. A touch burnt but clean. The mouth lacks amplitude but has character and botrytis flavour (rôti)." (l'Institut d'Œnologie de Bordeaux, 1978) ; "Exquisite scent of grapevine flowers, fringed with a discreet vanilla and completed by a smoky, charred note. A perfect harmony reigns amongst the rich essences that one divines there : no trace of heaviness, a supreme elegance. Myriad savoury nuances which form a whole from which no single one can be detached. A prolonged aerial distinction." (Robert Goffard, 1984). Picking began 2 October.

1954 : Fading. "Dark gold. Nice soft honeyed with botrytis." (Jeffrey Benson and Alastair Mackenzie, *Sauternes*, 1978). Picking began 4 October.

1955 : Great wine. All published notes for this vintage are studded with superlatives. "Very rich and complex nose with great finesse. Very full wine with lots of ripe botrytis flavour [rôti] and great class. Retains freshness. The ideal." (l'Institut d'Œnologie de Bordeaux, 1978). Picking began 21 September.

1956 : A light vintage, fading. "Amber gold colour. Subdued nose. Some vanilla and caramel. Nice flavour. Again, caramel and vanilla. Some acid on the finish." (*The Underground Wineletter*, 1983). Picking began 10 October.

1957 : Lovely wine in perfect balance, subtle, understated with subdued liquorous quality. Seems fuller and richer today than ten to fifteen years ago (1984). Picking began 30 September.

1958 : "A great Sauternes, full-bodied, silky. Highly developed bouquet. Not too sweet. Comes over well with foie gras." (*La Revue du vin de France*, 1978) ; "Light but elegant and very flavourful with nuances of vanilla, tropical fruit and some caramel. Good length on palate. Very nice." (*The Underground Wineletter*, 1983). Picking began 7 October.

1959 : Big rich wine marked by almond scent and flavour. "Deep, rich, magnificent bouquet, honeyed and fragrant, still very sweet, full-bodied, fat, concentrated wine."

(Michael Broadbent, *The Great Vintage Wine Book*, 1979). Picking began 21 September.

1960 : " Mid-gold, good rich nose, very good balance and finish. " (Jeffrey Benson and Alastair Mackenzie, *Sauternes*, 1978) ; " Rich, caramel and vanilla flavour. Drying out just a bit and a touch of heat on the finish but still nice. " (*The Underground Wineletter*, 1983). Poor notes from the Brussels tasting (1984). Picking began 2 September.

1961 : " Good Yquem vintage. Zest with long finish. Ageing potential : 70 years. " (Yquem, 1982) ; " Well-developed nose, very clean with great finesse. Lots of ripe botrytis flavour. Full-bodied. Very complex and harmonious. Good oak taste. " (l'Institut d'Œnologie de Bordeaux, 1978). Picking began 19 September.

1962 : " Sharp, fruity nose. Zesty and smooth. Beautiful finish. Great bottle. " (*La Revue du vin de France*, 1969). " Clean, well-developed nose. Good oak, very mature. Slightly acid and very sweet. Very rich and harmonious. Full-bodied. " (l'Institut d'Œnologie de Bordeaux, 1978). Picking began 2 October.

1963 : A poor year. Very little Yquem made. The wine deepened in colour rapidly and aged prematurely. On the decline. Picking began 4 October.

1964 : No Yquem. Picking 21 September–20 November.

1965 : Most notes indicate a pleasant, clean nose and little body. " Medium gold colour. Very subdued nose with a hint of tropical fruit and coconut. Light flavour of vanilla and coconut. Drying just a bit with acid on the finish but still nice. " (*The Underground Wineletter*, 1983). Picking 22 September–30 October.

1966 : " ... scent of jasmine ... burnt note ... full, very well-balanced with a fine spectrum of savours ... fresh, elegant, lacy. " (Jo Gryn, *Gault-Millau*, 1984). Picking 15 September–9 October.

1967 : " Burnished old gold ; scents of honey, amber, fresh-mown hay ; intense mellow richness, very full, unctuous. Very rich wine, great distinction, of a perfection approaching it to the '29 ; exceptional vintage. Ageing potential : more than a century. " (Yquem, 1983). Picking 26 September–25 October.

1968 : A difficult year ; only 10 per cent of the harvest was chosen to become Yquem. " Deep gold, nice complex honeyed nose, tight, firm with acidity, closed with life to come. " (Jeffrey Benson and Alastair Mackenzie, *Sauternes*, 1978). Picking 30 September–8 November.

1969 : " Young, clean botrytis nose, no volatile acidity, a bit acid and hard, not typical, somewhat lean. " (l'Institut d'Œnologie de Bordeaux, 1978). Picking 30 September–25 November.

1970 : " Wine for laying down. Slow ageing. Good balance. Should hold sixty years in a good cellar. " (Yquem, 1980). " Not much nose, has lost its fruit but hasn't much bouquet of mature wine. Full and supple, relatively non-acidic, full. No volatility. " (l'Institut d'Œnologie de Bordeaux, 1978). This note, which on the surface appears to be harsh and negative, is, in fact, the description of a very great wine in a temporarily muted stage of its development. Picking 25 September–24 November.

1971 : Another great success – more rapid evolution than the 1970 ; already open, fine drinking but with a splendid future. " Very agreeable, young fruity nose, no volatility.

Fat and voluptuous. Well-balanced, perhaps slight acidity on finish." (l'Institut d'Œnologie de Bordeaux, 1978). Picking 30 September–4 November.

1972: No Yquem. Picking 5 October–14 December.

1973: Fragile wine, delicate balance, lovely now. Picking 2 October–21 November.

1974: No Yquem. Picking 26 October–7 December.

1975: Great wine in the making. At present beginning to open up but still dense and quasi-impenetrable. Will provide wonderful twenty-first-century drinking. The following note, on the surface a bit negative, is a perfect description of a slumbering giant: "Oaky nose. No more fruit of young wine and not yet the bouquet of mature wine. Fat, a bit too luscious." (l'Institut d'Œnologie de Bordeaux, 1978). "Prototype of great Yquem; well balanced. Recalls the vintages 1937, 1945, 1953, 1955." (Yquem, 1980). Picking 29 September–7 November.

1976: All the grapes brought in on second *trie*. Beautiful voluptuous wine, much more forward than the 1975. "Lots of fruit, very good bouquet of young wine. Fat and rich, a bit too luscious." (l'Institut d'Œnologie de Bordeaux, 1978). " ... a sublime and extravagant liqueur." (Dr Emile Peynaud, 1982). Picking 21 September–13 October; the shortest on record.

1977: Light and elegant wine, perfect of its kind, for drinking in the decade to come. Better suited to foie gras or fish in sauce than a huge, voluptuous vintage. Picking 20 October–26 November.

1978: A well-constituted wine, slow to evolve, still jealous of its qualities and difficult to judge but presents no problems; a fine bottle for the 1990s. Picking 25 October–8 December.

1979: "An extremely elegant Yquem ... Its balance of flavours is already perfect ... Powerful without showing it ... persistent, lingering aromas of great finesse. It has the breeding and the distinction of its noble origin ... This vintage will always preserve a special charm to enrichen the savoury palette of Yquems." (Dr Emile Peynaud, 1983). Picking 15 October–29 November.

1980: Bottled in March 1984. Splendid quality. For laying down. The characteristics of the vintage fall between those of 1970 and 1971. Picking 20 October–18 November.

1981: Bottled in March 1985. "Harvesting conditions and the quality of the musts promise an Yquem of the highest level with a great ageing potential." (Yquem, 1983). Picking 5 October–13 November.

1982: Only the first two *tries* (before the rains set in) used for Yquem. Small quantity, expected to evolve into a great Yquem. Picking 16 September–7 November.

1983: In casks until early 1987. Expected to be a great, long-lived wine. Picking 29 September–18 November.

1984: Small harvest due to *coulure*. Because Yquem held off until late to begin picking, the quality of the wine is judged to be superior; 75 per cent retained for Château d'Yquem. Picking 15 October–13 November.

1985: In barrels until spring 1989. Unusual vintage. Reticent botrytis. Only 20 per cent retained for Yquem whereas half becomes "Y". Picking 1 October–19 December, the longest and the latest on record.

The most Expensive Wine in the World is not Expensive

The particular attentions demanded by Yquem, as well as its extremely limited production, have always imposed prices that seem high by comparison with other wines. Two centuries ago the United States consul in Bordeaux, no doubt closer to his purse and less impassioned by great wines than his future president, remarked to Thomas Jefferson that he was paying very dearly for his wines from Yquem. The 20,000 francs paid by grand duke Constantine in 1859 for a *tonneaux* of 1847 Yquem were, until that time, the record price for a wine. A bill, dated 1871, from Yquem's archives informs us that the wine of Château d'Yquem 1861 was sold from the property at three times the price of a first growth, the Château Coutet 1861, and at four times that of a second growth, the Château Filhot 1861, both of which were at that time properties of the Lur Saluces family.

PRICES AT AUCTION

The period beginning in the early 1930s that lasted until the end of the 1960s was one of continuing hard times for vineyard proprietors. Today the mood is euphoric. At the auction houses, of which Christie's in London sells the lion's share of old vintages of Yquem, it is hard to believe that, as recently as 1971, a prestigious vintage such as 1945 went for £ 8 a bottle whereas today the price of the same bottle at auction may be multiplied by 35 – and on restaurant wine lists by more than 100 ! In 1971, a case of Yquem 1962 was sold at Christie's for £ 41, or £ 3.40 a bottle ; in 1986 a vintage of similar quality and of the same age, the 1976, commands more than 20 times this price.

Amongst the old bottles of Yquem recently sold at auction are to be noted an 1817 (Leys, Antwerp, 1984) for 6,500 French francs, an 1858 (Christie's, London, 1984) for 6,800 francs, an 1861 (Sotheby's, London, 1985) for 5,500 francs, an 1865 (Christie's, 1984) for 8,300 francs, an 1893 (Hôtel Drouhot, Paris, 1984) for 5,500 francs, and a 1900 (Christie's, 1984) for 6,000 francs. At present, in the auction houses, the 1921s and the 1928s touch or exceed 4,000 francs a bottle and the 1937s and 1947s, 3,000 francs a bottle.

The price of a bottle of Yquem in a restaurant is often a question of the length of time it has spent in the restaurant's cellars. Thus, a 1904, Chez Hiély in Avignon, is listed at 1,900 francs; a bottle of 1904 was sold at Christie's on 30 May 1985, for £460 which, multiplied by three, would place the bottle on a restaurant wine list at about 14,000 francs (an 1893, at the Moulin de Mougins, is priced at 15,000 francs).

At Georges Blanc's, in Vonnas, from a beautiful suite of vintages, the oldest of which is 1890, the most expensive bottle is a 1921 at 9,600 francs; the lovely 1971 is listed at 1,000 francs. Chez Bocuse, the 1970 is 1,200 francs, the 1971 is 1,000 francs and the 1975 is 1,200 francs. At Troisgros the 1976 is listed at 1,000 francs, at the Moulin de Mougins at 1,070 francs and at Baumanière at 1,200 francs; at Baumanière, the 1975 is 1,300 francs, both the 1961 and the 1943 are listed at 3,000 francs and the 1937 at 4,000 francs. Elsewhere, it is not unusual to find the same bottles listed at double these prices.

Obviously, such figures ensnare one in reveries. And to add a bit of spice, journalists unhestitatingly invent fantasy variations on the theme – in June 1985, for instance, one of the important French weekly magazines reported that the 1983 Château d'Yquem was being snatched up at 800 francs a bottle when it could be found, whereas the 1983 is, in fact, quietly evolving in casks and will not be commercialized until after the spring of 1987.

Finally, it should never be forgotten that each time a bottle changes hands the price rises and that the greatest benefits are not those of the producer. To get out of the world of fantasy and return to solid ground, one must check prices with the Bordelais négociants, who are the first to handle Yquem. In March 1986, the 1981 vintage was sold to private individuals within France, with approximately 18 per cent tax included, at about 560 francs a bottle and the 1980 at about 520 francs. In fancy shops or at Parisian wine merchants, these same bottles vary between 700 and 850 francs and, on a restaurant wine list, depending on when they were bought, between 1,000 and 2,000 francs.

" At an age when one can hardly read, I was spelling out, drop by drop, delicate old clarets, dazzling Yquems. "
Colette.

NOTES

1. Beginning with the 1975 vintage, the citations " Sauternes Appellation Contrôlée " and " mis en bouteille au château " have been transferred from the label to a strip placed beneath it on the bottle, thus reinstating the virgin beauty of the pre-1920s labels. For reasons of presentation this strip has been removed from the bottle in the cover photo.

2. The " Rôles Gascons " are registers that were kept by the English Royal Chancellery of political and business affairs between England and Aquitaine, for the most part during the period of English rule. Those that remain are dated from 38 Henry III (1254) to 7 Edward IV (1468) and include nearly 2,000 skins of parchment, sewn end to end, divided into 144 *rôles* that are now housed in the Public Record Office in London.

3. The holdings of the royal provostship of Barsac, of which Yquem was part and of which the king, represented by the provost of Barsac, was " landlord ", were let to privileged persons on a feudal system known as *tenure roturière*, or common tenure.

4. La Fronde is the name given to the generalized revolt, 1648-1652, during the minority of Louis XIV (who was 10 years old at its begin-

nings) against the prime minister, Mazarin, and the queen-mother regent, Anne of Austria ; l'Ormée, so-called after the square planted to elm trees *(ormes)* in which the members of the group met, was the specifically Bordeaux opposition faction that kept anti-royalist activity alive until 1653.

5. Before the Revolution, itinerant military camps were stationed in the region of Saint-Omer-en-Chaussée, a village 90 km north of Paris.

6. The comte de Lur Saluces is presently in litigation with the Swiss cigar manufacturer, Davidoff, for having appropriated " Yquem " as a trademark for one of his cigars.

7. Jefferson's spelling was often aurally influenced ; " Sauterne ", spelt without the final " s " is, however, correct for the period, as is " Grave " instead of " Graves ". Orthography was more erratic at this time ; many authors refer to " Château-Iquem " throughout the nineteenth century.

8. Jefferson's available correspondence concerning Yquem is contained in vols 12-20, the last published volume of *The Papers of Thomas Jefferson*, published by Princeton University Press ; 40 volumes still remain to be published.

9. The figure of 66,000 which at present serves as the base upon which to calculate the sales of Yquem, will, in a few years' time, be closer to 72,000 thanks to the progressive increase in recent years – about 10 per cent in all – of the surface of vines in production ; this has been made possible by treating the soil with disinfectants, permitting a more rapid return to a biological balance than in the past. Moreover, the purchase, presently in negotiation, of 13 hectares (32 acres) of land in enclave or bordering the estate, of which half is *appellation contrôlée* vineyard with the same soil structure as that of Yquem, will increase the total vineyard area to about 109 hectares (270 acres). Thus, in some ten years' time, the average annual production should be stabilized, without any increase in production per hectare, at around 77,000 bottles.

10. Chaptalization : the addition of sugar to unfermented must to raise the degree of alcohol in the fermented wine, a practice that takes its name from Jean-Antoine Chaptal, Napoleon's Minister of the Interior, who recommended it as a corrective measure for dry wines in deficient years. It is now common practice in Sauternes.

11. Official legislation for Sauternes permits the somewhat

exagerated production of 25 hectolitres per hectare (267 gallons per acre) of "Sauternes A.O.C." (*appellation d'origine contrôlée*) ; a typically sly clause allows for an additional production, from the same vines, of a certain amount of "Bordeaux A.O.C.", variable from one year to another but normally around 10 hectolitres per hectare, an invitation to overproduction which most, but not all, of the classed growths reject.

12. Cited by Henri Redeuilh, "Notes sur l'ancienneté de la méthode des vendanges tardives et des 'tries' en Sauternais et à Sainte-Croix-du-Mont", in *Vignobles et vins d'Aquitaine* (Bordeaux, 1970). The document is in the Archives du département de la Gironde, reference : 3 E 6096.

13. Henri Kehrig, *Le privilège des vins à Bordeaux jusqu'en 1789* (Paris and Bordeaux, 1886).
L'année 1647. – Prix mis aux vins de la sénéchaussée et pays Bordelois (*Almanach vinicole*, 1870, p. 50 – 1 écu = 3 livres).

Prix au tonneau :
Graves et Médoc : 26 écus à 100 livres.
Entre-deux-Mers : 20 à 25 écus.
Côtes : 24 à 28 écus.
Palus : 30 à 35 écus.
Libourne, Fronsadais : 18 à 22 écus.
Guitres et Coutras : 18 à 22 écus.
Bourg : 22 à 26 écus.
Blaye : 18 à 24 écus.
St-Macaire et la juridiction : 24 à 30 écus.
Sauternes :
Langon, Bommes et Sauternes : 28 à 35 écus.
Barsac, Preignac : 28 à 100 livres.
Pujols, Fargues : 28 à 100 livres.

Cérons et Podensac : 24 à 30 écus.
Castres et Portets : 20 à 25 écus.
Saint-Emilion : 22 à 26 écus.
Castillon : 20 à 22 écus.
Rions et Cadillac : 24 à 28 écus.
Sainte-Croix-du-Mont : 24 à 30 écus.
Bénauges : 18 à 20 écus.

14. Cited by Christian Huetz de Lemps in *La Seigneurie et le vignoble de Château Latour*, ed., Ch. Higounet, (Bordeaux, 1974).

15. Auguste Petit-Lafitte, *La vigne dans le Bordelais* (Paris, 1868) : "La maladie de la vigne (oïdium) marked a really disastrous period, notably from 1853 to 1857. Château-Yquem, where (from 1847 to 1852) an annual average of 116 *tonneaux* were made, attained (from 1853 to 1857) an annual average of only 29 ! " (Yquem's average production today for the total amount of wine produced is about 90 *tonneaux* per year.)

16. Petit-Lafitte, *op. cit.*, defines Sauvignon as the *cépage des Graves* (by which he means the left bank of the Garonne, including Sauternes), "Sauvignon is to the white varieties what Cabernet is to the red varieties ; it forms the base of the Graves vineyards. To it Sauternes ... owes its body and its sap." Sémillion, he defines as the *cépage des côtes* (the right bank of the Garonne) but adds that "one encounters [it] also and in very large proportion in the Graves vineyards."

17. Columella, *De re rustica*, Book IV (XXIV, 16).

18. The extremities of the vinestocks – the tips of the arms –

grow imperceptibly longer each year, for to each is added, at each winter's pruning, a short section of the previous year's growth. Thus not only must the young vine be formed but, in order to confine it, as nearly as possible, to its predestined mould throughout its career, the subtly shifting, expanding, mature vinestock must be periodically re-formed by astute pruning, an overextended arm tip amputated while a providentially positioned sucker has been preserved to be pruned back, shortening and replacing the arm tip. Although usually barren itself, the branches that grow the following year from the eyes of a sucker will be fertile.

There are other reasons for reforming a vine : sections of the basic vinestock may die in an older vine, imposing the sacrifice of one of its arms and the re-forming of a new arm over several years ; a few moments of hail may not only destroy a season's harvest but may batter the rootstocks so badly that they will require creative, surgical pruning in the winters to come.

These general rules of pruning are necessarily very flexible for, with the passage of time, a vine increasingly imposes its own individual needs on the pruner. Amongst the older vines one occasionally finds a vinestock that retains only a single twisted and tortured original arm, often with a more recently formed arm sprouting from it ; others may over the years have formed three or four arms and the number of *côts* may vary from two, to as many as five or six.

19. High production, achieved by forcing the vines with fertilizers and by long pruning, lengthens the grapes' ripening season and lowers their sugar content, while at the same time they retain more acid. The volume is further increased

by limiting the number of *tries* and picking grapes only partially affected by noble rot. It is a vicious circle, for the increase in quantity is automatically accompanied by a decrease in quality and leads to the practice of chaptalization to replace the lost sugar and further increase the quantity. Chaptalization is permitted by legislation in the amount of sugar necessary to raise the potential alcohol level by two degrees, approximately 7.5 kg (16 1/2 1b) of sugar for a standard Bordeaux cask containing 225 litres (48 gallons). This results not only in a dilution of flavour but in a chemical imbalance in the musts : the relative amount of botryticine manufactured by the botrytis during the natural process of concentrating the grape sugars is diminished to the degree to which the musts have been artificially sweetened. The botryticine's property of inhibiting the action of the yeasts, completely blocking fermentation at a given point, is attenuated and a correct alcohol-sugar balance in the wine can only be achieved by artificially arresting or " muting " the fermentation with a relatively massive dose of antiseptic sulphurous solution.

20. The horizontal press, a highly perfected piece of equipment, whose efficacy has long since been proven in Champagne, is used for a few pressings each year, mainly to accustom the cellar workers to its use. It exerts a firm but gentle and progressive pressure very similar in effect to that of the vertical hydraulic presses. It consists of a revolving, elongated cylindrical cage of enamelled steel within which is an inflatable heavy latex bladder. Having been filled with the *vendange*, the cage revolves while the collapsed bladder slowly swells, pressing the grapes against the walls of the cylinder. For second and third pressings, the bladder is deflated, the packed pomace is pushed free of the walls and the cylinder is whirled to crumble it before the bladder begins to inflate again.

21. *Débourbage* : for the vinification of most white wines, in order to facilitate and hasten the wine's ultimate clarification, it is considered crucial to render the musts as nearly limpid as possible before the fermentation is launched, its churning, disruptive activity denying any further possibility of sedimentation. To achieve this, a sulphurous solution is added to the vat of freshly pressed juice ; its effect is to temporarily paralyse the yeasts, retarding the début of fermentation and giving the musts time to settle before the relatively clear liquid is decanted into casks to ferment.

22. " Y " : in 1959 a wine baptized " ygrec " (" Y "), " Bordeaux A.O.C. ", was launched on the market, putting to use wines that, by other standards, are perfectly balanced but that are insufficiently dense and rich to bring to Yquem its characteristic qualities. It is defined as a dry wine but its degree of dryness is relative. " Y " is an assemblage of 50 per cent Sauvignon and 50 per cent Sémillon, the latter selected amongst the casks of lighter wines or, in certain years, from wines whose grapes have been unaffected by noble rot. In 1978, for instance, botrytis was recalcitrant and very little Yquem could be made, but the quality of the wine was high and 40 per cent of the harvest became " Y " (in 1977, it was 50 per cent, in 1979, 30 per cent, and in 1980, 15 per cent). It is not produced every year (there was no " Y " in 1975, 1976, 1981, 1982 or 1983) for, amongst other things, a certain amount of wine, impeccable in quality but too lightly structured to become Yquem, and an unusual abundance of Sauvignon, a less dependable producer than Sémillon, are necessary to its production. It is a gentle, refreshing wine, a perfect apéritif with memories of Yquem in its bouquet.

Yquem's soil structure ; drawing reproduced
from La Vigne dans le Bordelais,
by Auguste Petit-Lafitte.

BIBLIOGRAPHY

Allen, H. Warner, *A History of Wine* (London, 1961).

Atheneus, *Banquet des Savans* (ed. Lefebure de Villebrune, 1789). *The Deipnosophists*, vol. 1 (ed. Gulick, 1927). *Les Deipnosophistes*, (ed. Desrousseaux, 1956).

Barennes, Jean, *Le Château d'Armajan-des-Ormes* (Bordeaux, 1920).

Benson, Jeffrey and Mackenzie, Alastair, *Sauternes* (London, 1979).

Bidet, M., *Traité sur la nature et sur la culture de la vigne*, 2nd edn. (Paris, 1759).

Boyd, Julian P., (ed.) *The Papers of Thomas Jefferson*, vols 12–20 (Princeton, N.J.).

Broadbent, Michael, *The Great Vintage Wine Book* (London, 1980).

Chaptal, comte, *L'Art de faire le vin* (Paris, 1819).

Chenaye-Desbois, de la, and Badier, *Dictionnaire de la noblesse* (1868).

Cocks, Charles, *Bordeaux et ses vins* (Bordeaux, 1850).

Columella, *De re rustica*, book IV.

Courcelles, M. le chevalier de, *Généalogie de la maison de Lur Saluces* (extract from *L'Histoire généalogique*) (Paris, 1825).

Dion, Roger, *Histoire de la vigne et du vin en France, des origines au XIXe siècle* (Paris, 1959).

Dormontal, Charles, *Sauternes, pays d'or et de diamant* (Bordeaux, 1930). *Florilège des grands vins de Bordeaux* (Bordeaux, 1931).

Dovaz, Michel, *Encyclopédie des crus classés du Bordelais* (Paris, 1981).

Féret, *Statistiques de la Gironde* (Bordeaux, 1889).

Féret, Claude, *Bordeaux et ses vins* (Bordeaux, 1982).

Francisque-Michel, *Rôles Gascons, transcrits et publiés*, vol. I, introduction (Paris, 1885).

Galet, P., *Cépages et vignobles de France*, vols 2 and 3 (Montpellier, 1958 and 1962). *Précis de viticulture* (Montpellier, 1970).

Guillon, Edouard, *Les Châteaux de la Gironde* (Bordeaux, 1869).

Guyot, Dr Jules, *Etude des vignobles de France, région du Sud-ouest*, 2nd edn. (Paris, 1876).

Higounet, Ch., (ed.) *La Seigneurie et le Vignoble de Château Latour*, 2 vols (Bordeaux, 1974).

Jullien, Camille, *Histoire de Bordeaux depuis les origines jusqu'en 1895* (Bordeaux, 1895).

Kehrig, Henri, *Le Privilège des vins à Bordeaux jusqu'en 1789* (Paris and Bordeaux, 1886).

Lacoste, P., *La Route du vin en Gironde* (Paris, 1948).

Lafforgue, Germain, *Le Vignoble girondin* (Paris, 1947).

Lur Saluces, Henri de, *Notice généalogique sur la Maison de Lur*, followed by a *Précis historique sur les derniers marquis de Saluces et sur la cession de marquisat de Saluces à la France en 1560* (Bazas, 1908).

Meller, Pierre, *L'Armorial du Bordelais*, vol. 3 (Bordeaux, 1906).

Muralt, Pierre B. de, *D.I.V.O. : Yquem* (Lausanne, 1978).

Odart, comte, *Ampélographie universelle*, 6th edn. (Paris, 1874).

P.-L.-M. (Chemins de fer), *Instructions pour le traitement des vignes par le sulfure de carbone* (Paris, 1878).

Petit-Lafitte, Auguste, *La Vigne dans le Bordelais* (Paris, 1868).

Peynaud, Emile (see also under Ribéreau-Gayon), *Connaissance et travail du Vin* (Paris, 1971). *Le Goût du vin* (Paris, 1980).

Pijassou, René, *Le Médoc*, 2 vols (Paris, 1980).

Redding, Cyrus, *A History and Description of Modern Wines* (London, 1833).

Redeuilh, Henri, " Notes sur l'ancienneté de la méthode des vendanges tardives et des 'tries' en Sauternais et à Sainte-Croix-du-Mont ", *Vignobles et Vins d'Aquitaine* (Bordeaux, 1970).

Ribadieu, H., *Les Châteaux de la Gironde* (Bordeaux, 1855).

Ribéreau-Gayon, J. and Peynaud, E., *Traité d'œnologie*, 2 vols (Paris, 1964).

Roudié, Philippe, *Le Vignoble bordelais* (Toulouse, 1973).

Sourget, A., *Le Tombeau de Pierre Sauvage et la pierre commémorative du Château d'Armajan* (Bordeaux, 1878).

ACKNOWLEDGEMENTS

My gratitude is, above all, due to comte Alexandre de Lur Saluces and to his wife, Bérengère, for the warmth and generosity with which I have been received at Yquem and for the ungrudging expenditure of time answering myriad questions.

To Henri Flammarion, connoisseur of works of art and fine wines, whose decision it was that this book should see the light of day.

To Pierre Meslier and to Guy Latrille, who imparted much useful information in the course of the book's evolution ; to professors Philippe Roudié and Jean-Bernard Marquette, from the University of Bordeaux, who provided me with precious historical information.

To Marie-Madeleine Facca, comte Alexandre de Lur Saluces's personal secretary, indefatigable researcher and supremely efficient link between Yquem and my work table.

To Monsieur and Madame Perromat-Machy, who lent me valuable documents concerning the history of Château d'Armajan.

To the connoisseurs and collectors of Yquem the world over who shared with me both their passion for Yquem and their tasting notes, evoking happy marriages between Yquem and the table : Doctors E.A. Jackson, G.B. Klein, Haskell F. Norman, Marvin C. Overton III and Nils Stormby ; Messieurs Robert H. Bacon, Alain Blanchy, Michael Broadbent, Philippe Brunon, F. de Cock, A.D. Daxhelet, Bipin Desai, Robert Goffard, Thomas H. Gregory, Jean-Paul Jauffret, Nathaniel Johnston, Tawfiq N. Khoury, Edward Lazarus, G. Legrand, H.J.P. Manassero, Alain Maurel, the prince de Metternich, Robert Mondavi, Paul Paris, Hardy Rodenstock, Jacques Rouet, J. Scheidegger, André Schwaar, Percy Simmons, Abdallah H. Simon, Alex Szogy and Geoffrey Troy.

To the *maîtres cuisiniers* and restaurateurs who shared recipes and memories linked to Yquem : Messieurs Jean Bardet, Georges Blanc, Paul Bocuse, Jean-Paul Bonin, Yannick Cam, Alain Chapel, Frédy Girardet, Michel Guérard, André Guillot, Jean-Pierre Haeberlin, Nico Ladenis, Louis Outhier, F.-A. Perret, Claude Peyrot, Henri Van Ranst, Pierre Troisgros, Roger Vergé and Pierre Wynants.

To Ghislaine Bavoillot, who brought together the authors of this book – Michel Guillard, Marc Walter and myself – and who was the vigilant overseer and catalyst, at table and at desk, of our combined efforts.

To Michel Lemonnier for unfailing moral support during the writing of this book.

To Jill Norman, my British editor, with whom I have worked closely on the British and American editions of *Yquem*.

To my sister, Margaret Olney McBride, my brother, James Olney, and my friends, Mary Garin, Kermit Lynch and Aubert de Villaine, all of whom have read and criticized the manuscript of *Yquem* in the course of its conception.

Credits